MEAD

EMILY STEAD

ULTIMATE
FOOTBALL HEROES

MEAD

FROM THE PLAYGROUND
TO THE PITCH

DINO

First published by Dino Books in 2023,
an imprint of Bonnier Books UK,
4th Floor, Victoria House, Bloomsbury Square, London WC1B 4DA
Owned by Bonnier Books,
Sveavägen 56, Stockholm, Sweden

🐦 @UFHbooks
🐦 @footieheroesbks
www.heroesfootball.com
www.bonnierbooks.co.uk

Text © Studio Press 2023

Design by www.envydesign.co.uk

Paperback ISBN: 978 1 80078 636 3
E-book ISBN: 978 1 78946 718 5

British Library cataloguing-in-publication data:
A catalogue record for this book is available from the British Library.

Printed and bound in Great Britain by Clays Ltd, Elcograf S.p.A.

3 5 7 9 10 8 6 4 2

To Jacob,
The megs master!

Emily Stead has loved writing for children ever since she was a child herself! Working as a children's writer and editor, she has created books about some of football's biggest stars, teams and tournaments for many a season. She remains a passionate supporter of women's football and Leeds United.

Cover illustration by Dan Leydon.
To learn more about Dan, visit danleydon.com
To purchase his artwork visit etsy.com/shop/footynews
Or just follow him on Twitter @danleydon

TABLE OF CONTENTS

ACKNOWLEDGEMENTS

My first thank you is to Bonnier Books UK for adding me to their Ultimate Football Heroes squad, for this new title in a series of books that continues to thrill young readers and football fans in their millions.

To every teacher, bookseller and librarian who has helped get the books into the hands of readers special thanks are due. And of course an extra-special mention goes to you, the readers and fans – without you there wouldn't be any Heroes.

I was hugely honoured to be asked to share the story of Beth Mead – a European Champion, no less! A footballer whose rollercoaster journey has catapulted her from playing on a bumpy village pitch to playing in some of the greatest stadiums in the world and becoming the golden girl of Europe. Alongside her fearless Lionesses, Beth continues to inspire a generation of young footballers to follow their dreams.

Long before these latest Lionesses first kicked a ball though, generations of talented women helped pave the way for women's football to grow into the game it has become today. Women like Lily Parr and Bella Reay who sadly never had the opportunity to play for an official England team, despite their lionhearted love of the game. Or Sylvia Gore and Sheila Parker who played in the first England match to be recognised by the Football Association, as late as 1972. And all the women who have since juggled studies, jobs and families, while entertaining crowds for little reward or, at times, none at all.

The fifty-year ban by the FA on women's football that so cruelly and unfairly affected generations of women and girls has meant that the game is today still playing catch-up to where it should rightfully be. But with our current squad of Lionesses who are still fighting to give all young people the same opportunities to enjoy the beautiful game, women's football is in the best hands. Lionesses, your legacy as champions is set to go far beyond your achievements on the pitch. Thank you.

CHAPTER 1

A NIGHT TO REMEMBER

6 July 2022, Old Trafford, Manchester
Women's Euro 2022 Group A match –
England vs Austria

At last, the wait was over. The thirteenth Women's European Championship – and biggest ever – was greeted by a fanfare of music and fireworks. Sixteen teams. Ten stadiums. And hundreds of thousands of fans.

With home crowds on England's side, the Lionesses would never have a better chance of winning the trophy. It was the biggest summer of their lives – one that could see their hearts broken or see them hailed as heroes. Whatever happened, their goal was to make the nation proud.

England's first opponents were Austria. Just a few months earlier, the two sides had met in a World Cup qualifier in Sunderland. It was a special night for forward Beth Mead, returning to the city where she'd first made her name as a teenage goalscoring sensation. She had so wanted to impress at the Stadium of Light, and thought she had won a penalty that could double England's lead, only to see the ref wave 'play on'. Maybe she'd have more luck in Manchester?

Old Trafford had been chosen to kick off the Women's Euros – the 'Theatre of Dreams', the fans called it. As Beth looked around the packed stadium, memories of her first visit there as a young girl came flooding back. She'd travelled there with her dad, Richard, to see her hero David Beckham in action for Manchester United. She remembered their seats were really high up, with lots of concrete steps for little legs to climb, but it was worth it when they reached the top of the family stand. Beth spotted the Number 7 straightaway on the enormous grass pitch below, running his hands through his floppy blond hair.

Now Beth had the chance to become a hero too, as part of a squad of twenty-three talented Lionesses. They could make history if they won the Women's Euros, their first major trophy.

Five teams had a good chance of winning – Spain, Sweden, France and Germany were all dangerous sides – but England's home advantage made them favourites. The tag of favourites usually brought with it a huge weight of expectation, but England's special coach Sarina Wiegman had a way of somehow soaking up all the pressure for them.

She knew what it took to win the trophy, winning the Euros the last time around with her native Netherlands.

England's players trusted her completely. 'If we work together and try our best, success should follow,' Sarina told her team.

Old Trafford had a carnival vibe, with flags waving, music blasting out through the stadium sound system and the fans in full voice. A Mexican wave rippled around the ground before the game had even kicked off! While the two teams warmed up, Beth blocked out the noise. She was purely focused on the game ahead.

And after sixteen minutes it was Beth who gave England a dream start. Fran Kirby spotted Beth's darting run into the box and lifted a clever pass over the Austria defence towards her. Beth controlled the pass on her chest with a perfect first touch, before dinking the ball over the keeper. Then suddenly it felt like time eased into slow motion. An Austrian defender lunged desperately to try to make a save, but the ball crashed up onto the crossbar.

Had it crossed the line? It was tight, but Beth was sure it had. She reeled away to celebrate with the fans. The keeper, Beth's Arsenal teammate Manuela Zinsberger, wasn't protesting. Still, the goal would be checked by the Video Assistant Referee.

Time dragged slower still until finally, *GOAL!* the screens around the stadium flashed.

'That was cold!' said Georgia Stanway, the first to

smother Beth in a happy embrace.

Beth hugged her back, grinning. Inside though, she felt far from cool. That made it fifteen goals in her last fifteen games. She was a player on fire!

The crowd thought so too, as they burst into song:

'Beth Mead's on fire,
Your defence is terrified . . .'

Once they had the lead, England found their rhythm, and pushed Austria deeper and deeper.

Midway through the second half, high-fives were exchanged as Fran, Ellen White and Beth were replaced by Ella Toone, Alessia Russo and Chloe Kelly, three Lionesses hungry to make their mark. What was so good about this squad was just how much talent they had – the players on the bench were just as strong as the starting eleven.

When the attendance was announced – 68,871 – the crowd roared again. Beth and the bench clapped too. *Wow!* A record for a Women's Euro game and it was only the first match!

At the final whistle, the players huddled together. Sarina would have to save her team talk for the dressing room – she had never heard a crowd as noisy as this before! Instead, the players joined the crowd to sing 'Sweet Caroline'.

Then it was time for interviews. The pitch-side journalists were keen to talk to the goalscorer. Beth was buzzing so much that she found it tricky to string a sentence together. The lights, the crowd, the music. . . What an amazing night it had been!

'It's beyond words,' Beth blurted into the mic. 'Our fans were incredible – they were our twelfth player!'

She was convinced they had helped suck the ball over the line for her goal! The most important goal of her life.

Interview over, Beth sprinted to find her family in the far stand. She desperately wanted to share this moment with her mum, dad and brother Ben. They had been her biggest supporters since the very start of her football journey. If you'd told six-year-old Bethany Mead that times like these lay ahead of her, she'd have likely screamed in delight.

Tougher tests would come, Beth knew that. But tonight felt as special as any night she'd known, and she was going to soak up every second.

CHAPTER 2

BALLET SHOES AND FOOTBALL BOOTS

One of Bethany Mead's earliest football memories was kicking a sponge ball back and forth in the hall with her dad. Beth would raise her chubby toddler arms above her head in celebration each time she scored a goal.

'Again! Again!' Beth begged.

'One last time,' smiled Dad. 'Then it's bedtime.'

It was the only way to tire her out, it seemed. Though Dad was usually frazzled first.

Beth was born in the seaside town of Whitby and the family lived in nearby Runswick Bay. Growing up there, sheep easily outnumbered people in the little fishing village and its neighbouring farms, but Beth loved it. Scampering along the beach with the salty breeze blowing in her face made her feel alive.

By the age of five, Beth had more energy than ever – she never stopped! A hobby was what she needed, so Mum enrolled her young daughter in ballet classes.

It became clear quite quickly, however, that ballet wasn't for Beth. The strange names of the moves, the pink slippers, the frilly tutu. She hated them all! And she was forever getting told off for distracting the other dancers. The only way to get her to behave was to bribe her with the promise of getting a family pet. First came a rabbit, Beethoven, but it was a dog that Beth really longed for.

'We'll think about it, but only if you try your hardest to pass your ballet exam,' Mum said.

Now Beth had a goal to work towards, there was no stopping her. She stubbornly practised her *plié* and her *revelé* until the day she came home with her certificate. And to Beth's delight, the Mead family soon welcomed a new addition – a Border Collie pup called Jess.

Beth gave up ballet after that. So, what was next?

When Beth turned six, Mum discovered a football club on the village field in nearby Hinderwell. Sessions ran every Saturday morning on a scruffy field that had one bare metal goal and no pitch markings at all.

'She's welcome to join in, but the boys can be pretty rough,' Phil the coach warned at Beth's first session. It turned out that Beth was the only girl.

'She'll be fine,' said Mum, who was looking forward to an hour of peace and quiet.

By the end of the session, Beth had proved that she could match the boys for both skill and strength. No one could bully her off the ball!

'She's got talent, your Beth,' the coach told Mum. 'And she's rougher than most of the boys!'

So, week after week, Beth came back to Hinderwell. The kids learned to weave in and out of molehills to avoid twisted ankles, while the only spectators were the sheep in the surrounding fields. To Beth, though, it could have been Wembley Stadium. She loved it from the first moment she set foot on that pitch.

Now that Beth was a real footballer, she needed a pair of boots. One weekend, she and Mum scoured the local car boot sale. And there they were. A pair of shiny blue-and-red Umbro boots with studs. They looked about the right size, so Beth tried them on.

'How do they feel, love?' asked Mum, prodding her toes.

'They're perfect!' smiled Beth.

It was the best 50p that Mum ever spent!

Once her parents could see that Beth had fallen in love with football, they agreed to buy her a kit for her birthday. Dad supported Manchester United and was delighted when Beth chose to follow in his footsteps.

'Like the poor girl had any choice!' Mum joked.

Unlike the tutu, Beth never wanted to take her kit off, so the muddy shirt, shorts and socks were quickly washed and dried each night when Beth was in bed. They would always be laid out neatly, ready to wear again the next morning.

Beth's favourite United player was David Beckham, a genius midfielder who could strike the ball like no one else. He was amazing for England too. And just like her hero, Beth was fast becoming a skilful player. She was strong with both feet and easily stood out in the training drills, but it was during matches where she shone the brightest. While most of the kids all followed the ball like the spectating sheep, Beth was always one step ahead. Instead, she would pick up the ball in space and more often than not, she would magic up a goal from nothing.

About a year after starting in Hinderwell, Phil took Dad aside. 'Beth's too good for us now,' he explained. 'It might be time to try the girls' academy up at Middlesbrough.'

Beth would always be welcome in Hinderwell, but a pathway in girls' football could take her game to the next level, Phil explained.

So, Mum and Dad presented the idea to their young daughter. It would mean a long trip to Middlesbrough, forty-five minutes there and back in the car each way.

Beth was nervous. She had never played with girls before. *What if they don't like me? What if I'm not good enough?* The thoughts raced through her mind.

In the end, she decided to give it a go.

Beth was a lively, bubbly child once you got to know her – her teachers could certainly vouch for that! But in new situations, you could have been fooled into thinking she was shy.

It didn't help that the girls at the academy were mostly two or three years older than Beth and they all seemed to know each other. Not one spoke to Beth.

They must think I'm such a baby, she told herself.

The worst part was the wait before the session started. As the other girls practised their fancy tricks and kick-ups, Beth didn't try to compete. Instead, she stood on her own, kicking her football against the wall for what felt like hours. *Left foot, right foot. Left foot, right foot.* Until at last the coach blew the whistle to begin.

Beth had always felt free playing football with her mates, unstoppable at times. Here, though, she found it hard to breathe. If she made a bad pass or a simple mistake, it felt to Beth like her whole world was ending.

Almost every week, she would run off the pitch to find Dad in the gallery, tears streaming down her face. A few kind words and a cuddle were usually all she needed to get through the rest of the session, but the joy she had felt at Hinderwell just wasn't there. It wasn't the same game she knew and loved, and she didn't feel part of a team.

'I don't belong here,' Beth told her dad between sobs.

'Just try your best,' he said. That was all he ever asked.

CHAPTER 3

CALIFORNIA DREAMING

One evening at training, Dad got talking to a man called Dave Scott. He'd seen Beth play a few times at Middlesbrough's Academy. She was a good player, but she never seemed happy.

'Would your daughter like to come and play with us at California?' Dave asked.

California JFC was less sunny than it sounded – it turned out the club was named after the road in Middlesbrough where Dave lived! They already had a boys' team and were looking for some more girls to form a new girls' side.

Even a couple of months in, Beth felt like she had never settled at Middlesbrough, so she agreed to go along to see if this girls' club might suit her better.

When the morning came around, though, Beth had changed her mind. She felt too anxious to even get out of the car.

'I'm sorry Dad, I just can't,' she cried, in floods of tears.

Richard could usually win his daughter round with a little coaxing, but that day Beth was being extra stubborn. Her unhappy time at Middlesbrough had made her dig her heels in even more. Despite her dad's efforts, Beth wouldn't join the girls.

Then came a lightbulb moment. Beth spotted a crowd of boys training further down the field. She had loved playing with the boys in Hinderwell and was desperate to feel that same joy with a football at her feet again.

'Can you ask if I can play with them?' Beth begged her dad. 'Pllleeeease!'

After a quick chat, the boys' coach agreed. The boys themselves didn't seem to mind either, so Beth got stuck straight in.

It was a decision she never once regretted.

California Boys was exactly where Beth wanted to be. She lived in their green-and-white-hooped strip most of the time and the only tears were happy ones. Beth's favourite memories were of the football galas, where teams got to play tournament matches all day long. The kids would spray their hair California-green and fuel up on pick 'n' mix sweets. *Good times!*

Her teammates grew to become good friends too; to the boys Beth was just another player, and they were glad to have her on their side.

Sadly though, there were still some who believed that girls shouldn't play football. 'They'll cry if they get tackled,' or 'They'll be rubbish compared to boys!' came the jeers. What was worse was that it wasn't just the kids – it often started with the parents of opposition teams. They'd whisper or snigger when they saw Beth warming up.

It was something that usually didn't bother Beth – she happily carried on and let her feet do the talking. People soon changed their minds once they'd seen her in action!

She wasn't sure why, but something felt different

about the time she played in a match at Hunmanby, another seaside village. As the teams warmed up, Beth's stress levels were beginning to rise too.

'This should be fun,' sneered one boy, pointing out Beth to his teammates.

'Playing against a little girl!'

Beth was almost always the smallest player on the pitch, the youngest too, but she never really stopped to think about it. 'If you're good enough, you're in the team,' the coaches always said.

The boy meanwhile was dark-haired and stocky, and could have passed for a secondary school pupil – he was at least a foot taller than Beth!

'Too easy!' said one of his mates, loud enough for Beth to hear.

Beth felt both cheeks burn red and her heart begin to race. 'I'm subbing off,' she cried.

The match was due to kick off any second!

But there was Dad, as always, with just the right words. 'What do we say?' he began, putting his hands on her shoulders. 'The bigger they are, the harder they fall.'

And just like that, Beth's worries melted away.

The Yorkshire Terrier in Beth took over after that. She snapped at the heels of the huge defenders and stood firm when they tried to push her off the ball.

Then came her chance to have the last laugh, when a ball looped over the heads of Beth and the dark-haired boy out towards the corner flag. It was a foot race to see who would get there first.

'Take her on, son!' the boy's dad yelled from the sidelines.

As both players slid into the tackle, there came a blood-curdling scream. Dad sprinted down the touchline towards his daughter, but he needn't have worried.

Beth sprang up unharmed with the ball at her feet and carried on her run. The boy meanwhile was still sprawled on the floor. A shared gasp passed through the crowd.

'Looks like you chose the wrong "little girl" to pick on!' said Beth with a wry smile.

The tackle proved a game-changer – California began to play confident, free-flowing football after that while the home team was running scared. It was a performance to be proud of!

When the match had finished, some of the parents went to shake Dad's hand. Talent was talent, pure and simple.

It was a memory that Dad used to cheer up his daughter for years afterwards, retelling the story if Beth ever started to wobble or ever began to doubt her abilities.

Her mentality changed that day too. Beth decided that if she could beat the big boys at their own game, she was ready to tackle whatever lay in store in girls' football. A transfer to California Girls was her next move.

CHAPTER 4

YOUNG LIONESS

Playing in a girls' team wasn't the nightmare Beth had imagined as it turned out – the girls at California were much friendlier. By now there were enough players to form a separate team from the boys. Dad helped out with the coaching too, which made the team feel like a little family.

In the space of a few months, Beth's confidence had soared. She was working hard on the pitch to become a better player too.

Passing.

Vision.

Shooting.

Movement.

These were all skills that came naturally to Beth. Now she was adding discipline, fair play and respect to her game, listening carefully to her coaches' instructions.

'We win as a team, we lose as a team,' they repeated. 'With everyone working for each other.'

When she was nine, Beth even felt ready to return to Middlesbrough, and sailed through a trial at their Centre of Excellence.

'We think you'll do well here,' Andy, a coach there, told the young footballer.

Beth was thrilled! This time she never looked back, and began playing for Middlesbrough as well as her beloved California Girls. Now she got to play double the football!

Training was twice a week at first and there were matches all over the county too. Mum took on extra work cleaning holiday cottages and waitressing to buy the petrol they burned through travelling hundreds of miles each week.

When Beth reached the under-12s age group, FA rules meant that Beth had to choose one team. She was sad to leave California behind, but knew that Middlesbrough was the right place to carry on her development as a footballer. It had the best facilities, the best coaches and the most talented players from all over the North-East – she couldn't turn them down.

That year brought more big changes outside of football for Beth too. The Mead family moved house from Runswick to Hinderwell and Beth had to make the step up to secondary school in Middlesbrough.

The largest town on Teesside, Middlesbrough was still not massive, but compared to the tiny villages she had known, it may as well have been London. It proved a difficult time for Beth, going from knowing every single face at Oakridge Primary School to knowing hardly anyone at all.

Her first day was the worst. Beth felt like she'd never fit in. She and Mum walked Jess the dog along the clifftops after school.

'Please don't make me go back,' Beth pleaded with her mum.

'You'll soon settle, love!' Mum promised. 'Give it time.'

Mum was right, of course. After a little while, Beth slowly found her feet at her new school. PE was the lesson she most looked forward to each week – she shone at most sports including hockey and cross-country, while her collection of football trophies and medals won with school and Middlesbrough grew each year. Beth felt happiest and most carefree on a sports pitch. There, she could be herself.

*

Beth's nerves were always there in the background though, ready to make an unwanted appearance, especially when she had to do anything out of her ordinary routine. When Beth was twelve, she faced her biggest challenge yet.

'There's an England camp coming up,' Andy told her one day. 'We've picked you to go for a try out.'

A trial for England! It was everything she had ever wanted, so why did the thought of it send her stomach twisting into knots?

On the two-hour car journey to Hull, Dad explained what Beth could expect. The standard of football would be higher than she was used to, but it would be nothing she couldn't handle.

'That's why the coaches picked you,' Dad said. 'They know you're ready.'

'Maybe,' Beth muttered, so he'd stop talking. She wasn't convinced he was right.

The first day was filled with a series of drills, designed to test the players' skills and technique. Beth tried to summon some excitement, but it was her least favourite part of football – she'd rather be dribbling around players than cones any day.

Then came the final day of the trial and the matches! Seven versus seven. This was her chance to show what she could do.

When the ref blew her whistle, it was like a switch had been flicked in Beth's body. With her sharp runs and clever crosses, Beth lit up the pitch. Each time a chance fell to her, she put it away. Four goals later, the Hinderwell Hotshot had a huge smile on her face. The England coaches were blown away!

Beth didn't have to wait too long for their decision – Dad pulled over to take the phone call on the drive home. Good news – Beth was in!

England want me. Me. Beth Mead! There were so many talented girls at the trial, just like her. Beth could barely believe it.

A letter arrived to confirm her place at the next training camp a few days later. The England crest with three lions was printed at the top of the letter and it was signed by the senior Lionesses' manager Hope Powell, once an England star herself.

Incredible! Mum and Dad must have read that letter out loud over twenty times.

They had always joked that Beth was good enough to play for England, but now it was actually happening. In real life! It was a proud moment for the Mead family.

The morning Beth was due to go, her bags were packed but she didn't feel ready. Panic had suddenly set in. She had never been away from home before – away from Mum, Dad and Ben. Feelings of dread and fear had replaced those first fizzes of excitement.

'I feel sick,' said Beth. 'Don't make me go.'

'Let's get you some breakfast and take it from there,' Mum said softly.

Beth's mum, June, knew she couldn't make her daughter do anything she didn't want to. She also knew that once Beth was at that camp running rings round the other players, she'd feel better again.

So, step by step, they worked through Beth's worries together. Deep breaths, hugs and talking through her feelings helped Beth feel well enough to go.

Sadly, the homesickness continued to simmer inside her for years afterwards. It was the same each time she had to go away with England. The night before would always trigger feelings of worry in Beth. One time she threw her whole kit in the bin, positive she wasn't going. A couple of hours later she began to feel better.

On each of those early camps, she wished she could fast forward through the drills and matches and be beamed back home to Hinderwell. Looking back, Beth wished she had let herself enjoy the experiences. She was there to play football after all, her favourite thing on the planet.

Beth's first proper match for England's youth side

came when she was fourteen. Germany against England! This time Dad flew out to Germany with Beth, so she didn't feel quite so nervous. England lost badly, which took some of the shine off her debut, but it was still the biggest milestone in the young footballer's short career.

Wisely, she didn't dwell on the scoreline for long. Every team could have an off day, she knew that. What was important was how they bounced back. If Beth and her teammates could learn from their mistakes, the next time they'd be stronger.

CHAPTER 5

STEPPING UP

Back at her club, Beth was desperate to get back into her goalscoring groove. But it wasn't going to be easy, Middlesbrough's next match was a tricky tie away to Sunderland. Worse still, a niggle saw her start as sub.

Sunderland started strongly, racing into the lead. Middlesbrough were missing their star striker. Luckily, Beth managed to shake off her injury in time for the second half.

Half a match is better than nothing, she thought to herself.

Keen to make up for lost time, Beth dribbled at goal, taking on one defender, then another, before arrowing a left-foot shot towards the top corner.

'That's going in!' gasped Dad from the sidelines.

And it did.

And when a Sunderland defender hesitated for a second too long, moments later, Beth swept her second shot in from the edge of the box.

'Go on, girl!' Dad cheered.

Then, *BANG – GOAL!* Beth gobbled up an easy tap-in, smashing the ball into the roof of the net. She had completed her hat-trick . . . in fifteen minutes.

With seconds to go, she grabbed her fourth to give Boro an unlikely lead. Then time was up! Her teammates threw their arms in the air, as the Sunderland players dropped to their knees.

Beth was a half-game hero! Her four fantastic strikes had inspired Middlesbrough to an epic 7–6 win.

As she went to celebrate with Dad, a man introduced himself as Mick Mulhern, head coach at Sunderland Ladies. He looked after their Girls' Centre of Excellence too. He'd heard reports about a brilliant young forward on the books at Boro, so had come on a scouting mission. He was glad what he'd heard was true.

'You're a fantastic talent, Beth,' said Mick. 'We'd

love to sign you when you turn sixteen.'

What an offer! It had come like a bolt out of the blue! Beth was bowled over. Some of England's finest players – Jill Scott, Steph Houghton and keeper Carly Telford – had all started out at Sunderland.

'Now they're Lionesses,' raved Beth to Dad on the drive home. 'They get to play at World Cups!'

Beth remembered when another young player had made the same move from Middlesbrough to Sunderland a couple of years earlier. She had been so pleased for Jordan Nobbs.

Switching clubs would be a big decision, but Beth had time to think it over. Meanwhile it was back to work at Boro, safe in the knowledge that nothing would change until her sixteenth birthday. She carried on playing with freedom, growing stronger and becoming more clinical in front of goal. She could destroy any defence now and was scoring sixty goals a season.

But as her big birthday grew closer, so Beth's nerves returned. Life was moving too fast! She was settled at Middlesbrough – why did things have to change?

After much door-slamming and more kits in the kitchen bin, Beth began to consider the move. Deep down, she knew she couldn't waste this chance to test herself at a higher level.

'Let's at least go once,' Dad suggested. 'See if you like it.'

'Okay, I'll go, but I'm not making any promises,' Beth said, giving in at last. It was so frustrating when her parents were always right!

The first time Beth trained with Sunderland things went well – much better than she had expected. Her new teammates made her feel like one of the team from the start.

'They're even giving me the Number 9 shirt!' buzzed Beth.

Decision made. Beth had taken an important next step on her footballing journey. She could be a superstar at Sunderland and was excited to begin this next chapter.

*

And so began a busy time in Beth's life. Being a women's footballer was everything she'd dreamed of, but it didn't pay like the men's game. In fact, she even had to pay to play. She juggled school and a part-time job washing pots and waitressing with football. She saved for weeks until she had earned enough money to buy a decent pair of boots. The brand-new Nikes were a cool £100.

With her new shooting boots, Beth smashed her first season at Sunderland. The Black Cats won the league and Beth bagged the Golden Boot with twenty-three goals. Their next season mirrored Beth's first, but this time she scored even more goals! Beth won back-to-back awards as Sunderland's Player of the Year.

Any time that wasn't taken up by football was spent working or studying, until Beth was old enough to leave school.

The season after that, the FA announced a new Women's Super League. Teams could apply to join the league, but Sunderland's bid fell short. They weren't rich enough to join the top teams like Arsenal and Liverpool. Instead, Manchester City grabbed the last spot. Sunderland were devastated, but the team worked hard and earned promotion the very next season. Beth was so happy, and it felt all the sweeter joining the WSL the hard way.

But in September 2014, there was an interesting development. The manager of Arsenal Ladies, Pedro Martínez Losa phoned, with an offer for the young striker to join the Gunners. Wow! Beth was on the radar of one of the best clubs in Europe! Their squad boasted a whole bunch of elite players – Kelly Smith, Rachel Yankey and Alex Scott were just some of their superstars. Jordan Nobbs had moved south from Middlesbrough to Sunderland, and then to Arsenal too!

It was a good offer, but Beth decided to turn it down. Too many doubts flew around her head.

'It's a big step up to the top league,' she told her parents. 'I wouldn't want to be stuck on the bench at Arsenal.'

This time, Mum and Dad agreed. She had unfinished business at Sunderland – they had only just been promoted.

Her decision to stay was rewarded that same

summer as Sunderland turned professional. Now the club had the money to offer Beth a big contract! She would train at the Academy of Light where the men's team trained too.

That season, Beth made rapid progress, scoring fourteen goals in the WSL, including two against Arsenal. It felt amazing! Her flying form saw her voted the PFA Young Player of the Year at the end of the season, ahead of Keira Walsh and Nikita Parris.

'Congratulations,' said Steph Houghton as she presented Beth with the huge golden cup.

'I can't believe it!' Beth replied. This was her coolest trophy yet!

She almost had to pinch herself to check that she wasn't dreaming, but this was her life now. Beth had made it – she was a professional footballer, playing in the same league as stars whose autographs she collected as a kid. Her years of hard work, never missing a session, were beginning to pay off.

CHAPTER 6

SILVER LINING

It wasn't just at her club where Beth was flying; the young striker was now a regular pick in the Young Lionesses squads each year. Since joining Sunderland, and playing alongside women much older than her, Beth had had to grow up fast. And while her nerves resurfaced every now and again, she began to enjoy going away on England camps at last.

Beth was eighteen when she represented England in an important tournament held in Wales. It wasn't exactly on home soil, but it was close enough. UEFA's Under-19 Championship pitted Europe's strongest nations against each other in that age group, with the four semi-finalists qualifying for the Under-20 World Cup the next summer.

England were in a group with hosts Wales, an improving Denmark and the toughest of the three opponents, France. *Les Bleuettes* had won the tournament twice before, while England had one title, earned by their current coach Mo Marley in 2009. Some of the squad from that year had just made their full Lionesses debut, including former Sunderland stars Jordan Nobbs and Lucy Bronze.

One day that could be me! The thought fizzed in Beth's mind excitedly. Following in their footsteps would be a dream! But first, she had to perform in Wales.

First up were France, in Llanelli.

'So who wants to come to Canada next year?' said Mo, before the match.

An enormous cheer filled the dressing room. Beth glanced around her, watching her teammates check their laces were tied and their socks were pulled up. These were friends she had grown up with, sharing a special journey together.

'Let's do this, girls!' Beth boomed, clapping her hands together.

Jess Sigsworth got the striker shirt against France, keeping Beth on the bench until late into the match. And while a goal didn't come Beth's way, her quality made England that little bit stronger.

Despite chances on both sides, including a second-half penalty for France, the match ended in a stalemate. England had their keeper to thank for that! It was a big point for the young Lionesses; France had had more of the ball, but England had stood strong, showing their character.

Next in Camarthen, England took on the hosts. This time Beth played the full ninety, with the striker scoring late in the game to help the Young Lionesses roar to victory. Wales 0. England 3.

A few days later, it was a similar story. Beth again led the line for ninety minutes, as England beat Denmark 3–0. Three games. Seven points. England had won the group!

Back in Camarthen, the football was fast and free-flowing in the Young Lionesses' semi-final against Finland. Coach Mo Marley studied her side proudly, it was an excellent team performance. Beth kept her shirt for the game, and repaid Mo's faith in her by scoring two brilliant first-half goals. She would have loved to have stayed on for her hat-trick, but with the score at 4–0, Beth was given a breather a few minutes before full-time. The striker had run her socks off!

Then came the final at the Parc y Scarlets in Llanelli, attracting a sizeable crowd of more than 1,000 fans. France were the favourites, having beaten Germany in their semi-final, but after the two teams' draw at the start of the tournament, England were feeling positive.

'Let's enjoy this match,' Mo told her team. 'There's a trophy at the end of it.'

France looked dangerous in the first half, with Kadidiatou Diani and Aminata Diallo causing double trouble down the left, but the Young Lionesses kept France out. And try as they might, England couldn't break down France's defence either. With the game still goalless after ninety minutes, extra time would be needed to decide the winner.

Then at last France's captain Sandie Toletti found the back of the net, before Diallo doubled their

lead with a rare header. *Les Bleuettes* had spared
themselves the pain of a penalty shoot-out, earning
their third title in extra time.

English hearts were broken, but the girls had played
with passion and pride. With silver medals around
their necks, the Young Lionesses could return home
with their heads held high. There was another silver
lining for Beth too – her three goals in Wales had
won her the Silver Boot. It was a nice bonus, but
she would have swapped it for the team trophy in a
second.

*

Thanks to Beth's eye for goal and her positive
performances, her plane ticket to Canada for the
Under-20 World Cup was booked! Most of the squad
from Wales were going too.

With the best teams in the world battling it out
though, this time the tournament proved much
trickier. Nigeria and South Korea advanced from
Group C, while England in third place made an early
exit.

Beth only scored once, but it was a strike that

truly announced her talents on the world stage; her piledriver from forty yards out saw jaws drop all over the stadium! It was later voted the third-best goal of the tournament. The first player to congratulate Beth was seventeen-year-old Leah Williamson.

'Take a bow, Beth!' Leah said with a grin. 'There was no stopping that one!'

And while England couldn't reach the final eight, the experience of playing in a big tournament would carry the Young Lionesses far. There was a strong team spirit in the camp and plenty of positives to take away. These players were more than just teammates now, they were good friends too.

On the flight home, Beth's thoughts began to unravel. After living in each other's pockets for weeks now, this might be the last time the girls all saw each other for a while. When they landed back in England, they would all return to their own clubs up and down the country. With Beth being the only player from the North-East, Sunderland suddenly felt very far away.

CHAPTER 7

MAJOR MOVE

After three seasons as a Sunderland hero, it was time
for Beth to move on. When Arsenal came calling for
a second time, Beth knew it was where she should
go next. The timing was right for Sunderland too –
Beth had a big contract with the Black Cats, but they
couldn't afford her wages now that the men's team
had been relegated from the Premier League.

So Beth became a Gunner, taking a deep breath
before packing up her life and moving to London.
She was glad she didn't have to live in the middle of
the city. Instead, she was given a room in a house in
a small town called St Albans, near Arsenal's training
ground. Most of the players lived close by and the

town was surrounded by countryside not that different from her hometown of Hinderwell.

Although Jordan Nobbs and Katie McCabe were her new housemates, Beth's first weeks down south were a lonely time. An ankle injury limited her time on the pitch, which only added to her homesickness.

'Mum, I want to come home,' Beth would cry on the phone.

She knew there was no going back, though. What would she do? She came with a price tag too high for Sunderland now – it would mean giving up football altogether. Growing up was tough!

'One day at a time,' Mum said. 'Remember why you moved.' It was heartbreaking to hear her daughter so upset when she was 200 miles away. All she wanted to do was to give Beth a big hug! But the family had decided together . . . Arsenal had offered Beth the chance to follow her football dream, it was where she was supposed to be.

After a few tricky months, Beth made the Number 9 shirt her own. And once she had scored her first Arsenal goal, she couldn't stop! She loved playing at

Meadow Park and would happily stay out long after matches, signing autographs or taking selfies with every fan who asked.

Her bond with her teammates was growing stronger each week too. But then came disaster! In a one-on-one with the keeper in training, it was Beth who came off worse. A broken collarbone meant surgery and a second spell on the sidelines. Beth was miserable, but always kept the end goal in her head – to get back on the pitch for Arsenal.

She had only just returned to training when Arsenal announced another star signing. Two years younger than Beth, Vivianne Miedema was one of the hottest young strikers in the world. All the top clubs had been interested in Viv – she was the top scorer in the Champions League – but it was Arsenal who had won her signature. Unsurprisingly, the Dutch star went straight into the team.

Beth didn't handle being benched too well. 'I can't understand why they've signed her,' she told her dad on the phone. 'They've only just bought me.' *Am I not good enough?* she wanted to add.

'You're a fighter, Beth,' Dad replied. 'It won't be easy, but you've got to fight for your place.'

And there definitely was a place for Beth in the team, just not where she had expected. The coach Pedro called Beth over in the next training session.

'How do you feel about playing on the wing?' Pedro said cautiously. He knew the idea might not go down well.

'Me, a winger?' Beth replied. It flashed through her mind that Pedro might be playing a prank.

But the coach was serious. He explained about the role he wanted her to play.

Beth left training that day with her thoughts spiralling. *I've been a striker FOREVER. Goals are my bread and butter! How am I going to score stuck out on the wing?*

Then she weighed up the positives . . .

She knew exactly the sort of passes strikers liked.

She would still get to be on the ball lots.

She could cut inside and beat defenders too.

Maybe I wouldn't make such a bad winger? Beth pondered. Besides, Pedro only wanted the best for the team.

So Beth worked tirelessly to adapt her game and win her place back in Pedro's first eleven. Like Dad had warned, it was far from easy, but before long it felt natural – like she had always been a winger. And as long as she was on the grass, she was happy. She would have played in goal if she'd had to!

Although Beth got to grips with her new position, Pedro didn't last much longer in his. A slow start to the season saw Arsenal swap managers, bringing in Australian Joe Montemurro. Pedro's sacking took the girls by surprise, but results hadn't been good enough – something had to change. Manchester City had won the treble last season, to the envy of the rest of the league.

With Joe in charge, Arsenal soon looked sharper and hungrier for success. It was time to start winning some silverware.

In Joe's first season, the Gunners reached the league cup final, beating Manchester City. Goal: Viv, assist: Beth. Then they booked a trip to Wembley, to contest the Women's FA Cup final, where they faced Chelsea.

'Let's win this for the fans,' said the skipper Kim Little, geeing up her teammates in the tunnel.

An enormous crowd of over 45,000 fans were at Wembley that day to watch the two London sides battle it out. Not one player on the pitch could have dreamed of such a grand occasion whtn they were growing up – days like this just never happened in women's football. Slowly but surely, the women's game was growing.

Sadly, however, the day ended in defeat for Arsenal. The Blues showed their experience and played with more passion.

Chelsea's Ramona Bachmann smashed home top right. 0–1.

And bent the ball top left next, after a mazy run. 0–2.

Viv pulled one back after Beth's trickery on the wing. 1–2!

Before a moment of magic from Fran Kirby. 1–3 final score.

Beth found herself going through the motions after the match. Shaking the hands of the winners,

clapping the fans guiltily, collecting her runners-up
medal . . . she hated being on the losing side. She
would learn from this experience and move on,
hopefully to happier times.

CHAPTER 8

FRESH START

Beth had always imagined her first England camp to be a magical experience. Lining up alongside legends, seeing her name in the newspapers . . . for most players it would be a highlight of their football career. Something to look back on once they'd hung up their boots for good.

Beth had played in every age group for England's youth teams and was keen to make the step up to the senior squad. True, she hadn't been a professional footballer for long, but she felt sure she could do a job for England. But when her first call-up did arrive, what happened next left the fresh-faced forward feeling flat.

It came in October 2015, while Beth was still playing for Sunderland. Earlier that year she had become the youngest ever winner of the Golden Boot, aged twenty, after scoring for fun against some of the top teams in the league. That must have put her on England's radar!

Later that month, the Lionesses were due to travel to Shenzhen for the Yongchuan International Tournament, a friendly tournament of three teams – host nation China, Australia and England.

Many of England's top players ruled themselves out of the trip to play in the league cup final back home, so Beth was hurriedly added to the squad by boss Mark Sampson. She was ready to step up and shine, but she didn't feel wanted. It felt like she was only there to make up the numbers.

The flight to China took fifteen hours each way, the hotel and food were awful, and Beth wasn't given a single minute on the pitch. Still, she had loved training alongside some of her country's best players, and hung on to every bit of advice they offered.

Sampson never picked her again. Beth wasn't quite

sure why. He couldn't use the excuse of her being a lower league player, as Sunderland were now playing the top flight, the Women's Super League. Beth was beating the best defenders, week in, week out and racking up the goals.

Then at last, three years on from her disappointing false start with the Lionesses, things changed suddenly. Sampson had been sacked.

Beth didn't feel sorry for Sampson when she heard the news. Thoughts began to swirl in her mind: *This could be my chance to become a Lioness! There's a World Cup next year too!* She had never once given up on her dream of playing for England.

A few months later, the new coach was announced, creating quite a stir in the media. Phil Neville's record as a player spoke for itself – he'd won half a dozen league titles and the Champions League with Manchester United, and had over fifty caps for England's Three Lions too. But as a young manager, he still had everything to prove. And even more to learn about the women's game.

Not long into the job, Phil phoned Beth to

introduce himself.

Beth answered the call as soon as she saw his name on the screen.

'I like your game,' he told the young forward. 'But you'll need to keep working hard to break into this squad.'

Wow! Beth gasped, after hanging up. He wasn't trying to put her off – the conversation was exactly what she needed to hear. She had to bring her best game. Sure, there were talented players such as Nikita Parris, Toni Duggan and Fran Kirby ahead of her right now, but Beth was getting sharper and fitter with each season she played. She was ready to do whatever it took for the chance to become a Lioness.

Phil and the England coaches kept a close eye on the Arsenal winger, and not long after their first conversation, the call-up came. Beth was included in the squad for Phil's first home match in charge in Southampton. Over 25,000 fans were expected at St Mary's Stadium, keen to see the Lionesses beat neighbouring Wales in an important World Cup qualifier.

As expected, England battered the Welsh goal, but luck wasn't on their side that night. The Wales keeper was having the game of her life, making save after save after save!

Phil tried to boost his attack with a double substitution after fifty-four minutes, bringing on forwards Nikita Parris and Jodie Taylor. Only one more sub could be made.

Time ticked on with the game still goalless, until there were just ten minutes left to play.

I guess my debut will have to wait until another day, Beth told herself.

Then, at last, Phil signalled to the bench.

'Get ready, Beth,' he called. 'Let's see what you can do.'

Beth's legs jiggled as she stripped off her tracksuit. *Don't do this to me now!* she said under her breath. She hadn't felt nerves like these in a long time.

Jordan welcomed Beth onto the pitch with a high-five. 'Enjoy it!' she smiled.

Beth's confidence grew with each touch of the ball and each run she made, but the full-time whistle came in a flash. She hadn't managed to score, but it had felt amazing to make her debut. As always, Mum and Dad were in the stands – they wouldn't have missed this match for the world.

It wasn't until she was back in her hotel room that night that it finally sunk in. *My first cap – I'm a Lioness now!* Even ten minutes on the pitch had been a buzz – Beth had savoured every second. She hoped she wouldn't have to wait too long for her next opportunity.

CHAPTER 9

TIME TO BELIEVE

Beth must have done enough to impress against
Wales, as she made the bench for England's next
two matches, tricky fixtures away to Bosnia and
Herzegovina and to Russia. Even as a senior Lioness,
Beth still felt terribly homesick, so she was glad to
have at least one of her clubmates – first Jordan, then
Leah – to travel with. The Lionesses returned with
six priceless points to top their World Cup qualifying
group.

It was September 2018 when Phil gave Beth the
news she'd been longing to hear.

'We're away to Kazakhstan next,' Phil began. 'You'll
be starting the match.'

Phil was giving a few of his young players a chance – Leah Williamson was making her full debut too, while Keira Walsh was standing in as captain, aged just twenty-one. Phil didn't see it as a risk; he was trusting in his squad's energy, skill and youth to win the match.

Beth made a flying start, stepping up to score a penalty in the opening minutes to give England the lead. She saw another penalty strike the post, but grabbed her second goal by chipping the keeper with a neat first-time shot.

Phil was full of praise on the flight home. 'That performance showed exactly why I picked you,' he said. 'You're fast, fearless . . . and you can finish.'

'Thanks, gaffer!' Beth beamed proudly.

England had won 6–0, Beth had scored not one but two international goals, and now the Lionesses were heading home on a swanky business class flight. Beth had been on cloud nine since the final whistle!

*

The next match with England was Beth's biggest test yet. If the Lionesses could win this, they would qualify for the World Cup in France the following summer.

Phil, dressed for the occasion in a three-piece suit, took his place on the touchline in Wales.

'He thinks he's Gareth Southgate!' teased Jill Scott, as the teams warmed up.

'Does that mean we'll reach the World Cup semis too?' Steph Houghton said, smiling.

Like most of the girls, Beth had watched all of England's matches at the men's World Cup the previous summer. The Three Lions had been far from favourites before the competition, but Southgate's young squad had come within a whisker of making the final, uniting the nation along the way. If the Lionesses could match those performances, it would be a tournament to be proud of.

Toni Duggan, Jill and Nikita Parris all scored in the second half, as Beth cheered on from the bench. 3–0. England had done it – they had beaten Wales to earn their World Cup place, with a game to spare.

Back in the dressing room, hugs were exchanged and the music was turned to loud, as the Lionesses kicked off the celebrations.

'FRANCE, HERE WE COME!' shouted captain Steph.

'Phil's waistcoat was our lucky charm!' cheered Jill.

Beth giggled. Jill played the role of team joker like a pro. She exasperated the staff by always being late to meetings or losing her kit, but she was brilliant at lifting team spirits and helping to settle new players into the squad. Jill's seat on the plane was almost guaranteed. The Lionesses legend had already been to three World Cups!

I'd be happy just to play in one! Beth thought to herself.

But there were no guarantees that Beth would be going to France. She had only played in a handful of matches so far and knew that she still had plenty to prove.

*

The SheBelieves Cup is an annual tournament hosted by the United States, where four strong teams battle it out to win a trophy. Whoever won in spring

2019, would get a taste of silverware before the big one that summer – the World Cup.

Beth was thrilled when she learned she was in the squad. With Brazil and Japan joining England in the USA, she would face some of the toughest opponents in the game. Marta and Formiga for Brazil, Carli Lloyd and Tobin Heath for United States, and Saki Kumagai for Japan . . . all legends! It would be an honour to even share the same pitch as them!

England's first match was against Brazil, played in Chester, Pennsylvania, with the temperature hovering just above freezing.

'Perfect conditions for us!' Beth joked to Lucy Bronze, as the pair worked on their pre-match stretches.

'The Brazilians will be frozen solid!' said Lucy, smiling.

Both Beth and Lucy had grown up on the north-east coast of England, playing in every type of weather imaginable. The cold didn't bother them!

The game itself, though, took a while to warm up.

Both teams were nervy, with little free-flowing football being played. Sloppy passes, leggy runs, England were lacking their usual energy. Was it down to jet lag? They went in at half-time 1–0 down to a soft Marta penalty.

After the break though, Ellen fired back. Soon Brazil were on the back foot.

'Go win this for us,' said Phil, sending Beth on from the bench.

'Got it, boss,' Beth replied.

Less than ten minutes later, Beth picked up a pass from Fran out wide on the right wing.

The angle's tight, but not impossible. The footballing part of Beth's brain took over, as she struck the ball instinctively with her laces.

The whole stadium stopped as the ball sailed into the top corner. The keeper was nowhere!

'Stunning!' said the TV commentator. 'Absolutely stunning from Arsenal's Beth Mead!'

'That's our girl!' cried June Mead, leaping off her sofa.

Back home in Yorkshire, it was the middle of the

night, but Beth's mum, dad and brother Ben wouldn't have missed the match for the world.

'Was that a shot?' gasped Ellen, giving the winger a huge hug.

Beth just smiled modestly, before the rest of the team piled on. You only had to look on YouTube for proof of Beth's ability – she had a whole back catalogue of sensational strikes by now.

The goal proved England the worthy winner against Brazil, but Beth wasn't stopping there, another fine strike followed in England's victory over Japan. Two wins and a draw with United States saw the unbeaten Lionesses clinch the SheBelieves trophy for the first time. England had delivered against some top teams, with Beth one of their players of the tournament.

Beth was hitting her best form at the perfect moment, showing everyone what she was capable of. Was it enough to earn her a place in England's World Cup squad? It was time to start believing.

CHAPTER 10

2019 WOMEN'S WORLD CUP

It was early May when Phil announced his squad for the World Cup that summer. Trimming it down to just twenty-three Lionesses had given the England coach a major headache – there were so many strong players to choose from, who were playing for clubs in the top leagues of England, France, Germany, Spain and the USA. One player who sadly wouldn't be on the plane, though, was Beth's Arsenal teammate Jordan Nobbs, who was out with a serious knee injury.

Beth was home alone when she opened her email from the Football Association. She didn't want to jinx her chances. Her eyes scanned the screen searching desperately for one word. . .

'CONGRATULATIONS.'

'I'm in!' she screamed out loud. Beth was going to France!

It shouldn't have come as too much of a surprise – she'd been one of Arsenal's best players that season, as the Gunners were crowned league champions with a game to spare. She had scored eight goals and made more assists than anyone else in the league. Beth had plenty to offer England.

'I can't believe it's really happening,' she told her family, bursting with a mix of pride and disbelief.

Now all she had to do was persuade Phil to put her on the pitch.

It worked! Beth would make her World Cup debut in England's first match against rivals Scotland. She was starting on the left wing, while her captain at Arsenal, Kim Little was on the opposition.

In the sunny stands of the Stade de Nice, her family were ready with their flags. England dominated the first half and went in 2–0 up at the break, thanks to goals from Nikita and Ellen. But it was Scotland who came out fighting in the second half, pulling a goal back. The game ended 2–1, giving England a narrow victory.

'We've got the three points,' captain Steph told her team in the post-match huddle. 'That's all that matters.'

After the match, Beth dashed to find Mum and Dad. They couldn't have been prouder!

'I'm just getting started,' she told them, with a big smile on her face. Now she had to make the teamsheet for the next game.

Next up were Argentina, the weakest team in the group. Beth got her wish and started on the left wing again – here was her chance to shine.

In a fiery match, England tested the Argentina keeper again and again, until at last, they scored. Beth and Jodie Taylor were sharing a room in France and had been working hard together in training too. Beth knew exactly where to deliver her cross for Jodie to slam the ball into the back of the net. And their plan went perfectly. *Gooooaaaalll!*

The match ended in another narrow win, but England's six points meant that they were through to the Round of 16 with a match to spare.

There was disappointment for Beth though – Phil was resting her for the next match.

I don't need a rest! I need to play! Beth wanted to say. Instead, she kept quiet and vowed to be ready and waiting if England needed a super sub.

England looked much more comfortable against Japan, with two goals from Ellen sealing their place as group winners. Beth watched the whole match from the bench. She didn't get on in the Round of 16 either, where England thrashed Cameroon 3–0. But although Beth was disappointed to miss out on the games, she was called on in the quarter-final.

The Lionesses were already 2–0 up by the time Beth joined the action against Norway, but she was determined to make an impact. Her chance soon came when England were awarded a free kick in a dangerous area. The Norwegian defenders expected a deep ball into the box, but Beth had other ideas – she'd spotted Lucy unmarked on the edge of the area. The pinpoint pass dropped perfectly onto Lucy's boot, as she smashed home a vicious volley. BANG!

England were through to the semi-finals of the World Cup! Only one team now stood in their way to the final. Unfortunately, that team was the United States, three-time winners and the reigning champions.

They'll be tough to beat, sure, Beth told herself. *But nothing is impossible in football.*

England knew they had to put on a show for the 50,000 fans packed inside the Stade de Lyon. Thousands of fans wearing face-paint and waving St George flags were there to cheer on the Lionesses – England had to use their energy.

Phil was impressed with Beth's assist against Norway and put her back in the first eleven. Beth wasn't going to waste her big chance.

'I'm ready,' she promised him.

With both teams looking to take charge of the game, it was the USA who went ahead through a Christen Press header.

'Let's stay switched on,' Steph shouted, clapping her hands together.

Minutes later though, Beth spotted Ellen's run

to the near post and sent over a fabulous cross for England's Number 9 to bury. Ellen was unstoppable – it was her sixth goal of the tournament.

'What a cross – it was on a plate for me!' Ellen thanked her teammate.

Now the scores were level, the game was there for the taking. The next goal would be key. Sadly for England, it was scored by Alex Morgan, who put USA back in front with a powerful header. Beth left the field with England 2–1 down, hoping Fran Kirby's fresh legs would make the difference.

It wasn't to be though – England's luck had run out. Ellen scored again, only for it to be ruled *offside* by a toe, before winning a penalty that Steph sent straight into the keeper's arms. A red card for Millie Bright ended all hopes of an equaliser after that. United States were worthy winners and would go on to win their fourth title.

England were out, but this squad of brave Lionesses had given the fans plenty to sing about in France. They returned to England having made a nation proud – almost twelve million people had watched England go toe-to-toe with USA on TV. A new record!

Beth could be proud of her own performances at her first major tournament too. It was frustrating that England had come so close to making the final, but she could go home to Hinderwell with her head held high.

Back at her family home, Mum showed her all the newspaper clippings she'd been saving, from the national and local papers too. Beth sat at the kitchen table reading through all the stories.

Wow! Fans up and down the country had fallen in love with the Lionesses! She felt so proud of the squad's achievements together. This wasn't the end, though, far from it. These players were special – they would be ready next time. England would go again.

CHAPTER 11

A FACE THAT DIDN'T FIT

After the World Cup, the Lionesses found it hard to hit their top form again. Some poor performances saw England slump to eighth place in the world rankings.

Spring 2020 saw United States take back the SheBelieves Cup, a tournament that turned out to be Phil Neville's last as England's head coach. His time with the side had finally fizzled out.

Beth wasn't sure what to feel. On one hand, Phil had given her the chance to make her debut and always believed in her, but he hadn't managed to get the best out of his talented squad. Superstar coach Sarina Wiegman was announced as Phil's replacement, but first she had to take the Netherlands team to the Olympics that summer.

Until then, Hege Riise would manage England, then Team GB at the Olympics. As a player with Norway, Hege had won every trophy going. A World Cup, a Euro championship and an Olympic gold medal. She had once been the best player in the world! After that, she had helped coach the United States.

But when Hege's first England squad was revealed by email, Beth hadn't made the cut. No reason given – just that she hadn't been picked this time. In the end, Beth did go to the camp, for the injured Fran Kirby, but she was made to train in defence.

How can I show what I can do if I'm played out of position? Beth wondered.

It didn't seem fair, but Beth took on the challenge. No one could ever say she didn't work hard.

There's still a place in the Team GB squad up for grabs, she told herself.

Making that squad would be tougher still – only eighteen players would go to Tokyo. Hege could easily select an amazing squad from only Lionesses, but now Scotland, Wales and Northern Ireland players were in the mix too. Even so, Beth believed she was good enough.

On the morning of the squad announcement, Jordan called. She hadn't been picked.

'I'm gutted,' she said. 'Fingers crossed for you, mate.'

Now the panic set in. Beth had a bad feeling. *If Jordan's not good enough, are they really going to choose me?* she worried.

Hours passed before Hege finally phoned Beth. The conversation lasted just a couple of minutes. Hege was abrupt, businesslike. Beth wouldn't be going to Tokyo.

It felt like a body blow. Beth dropped her phone on the table, her hand shaking.

'I can't believe it,' she snapped to her dad. 'I'm not even a reserve.'

'It's just one tournament,' Dad tried to reassure her. 'The new season will be here before you know it.'

He was right. Get through the summer and Beth could start afresh. Arsenal had another new coach and Sarina would finally take the reins as England boss.

But Hege's rejection stung. *How am I supposed to*

feel seeing all my teammates jet off to Japan without me? Staying angry would do no good, but Beth couldn't shake her black mood.

The Team GB squad was made official the next day. Three Arsenal players were in: Leah Williamson, Lotte Wubben-Moy and Scotland player, Kim Little. Keen to understand why she wasn't the fourth, Beth asked for a video chat.

Hege revealed that Beth's player report card had counted against her.

Report card? I'm a professional footballer, not a schoolkid! Beth wanted to say, but she managed to hold her tongue.

'It says you're too aggressive,' Hege read her notes without emotion.

What? The words hit Beth like a tackle from behind. *I've played some of my best matches when I've been angry! Everyone says so!* she silently raged.

When Hege hung up, Beth felt terrible. She racked her brain, trying to think of a time when her aggression – her commitment – had cost her team. She'd been sent off once for Arsenal that season, but even that should have been a yellow card.

Then the penny dropped: *My face will never fit while Hege is coach,* Beth realised.

So, Beth took the summer off and some time out from the women's game. She didn't walk away from football completely though – when England's men reached the Euro final against Italy, Beth and Jordan snapped up some tickets for Wembley.

What a buzz! Beth had forgotten how much she loved being a fan. Along with the pain that came with it . . . England crashed out in a penalty shoot-out, but the boys had given everything. The Three Lions had united the nation!

Legendary Lionesses Kelly Smith and Casey Stoney were sat a few rows away. Both had bounced back from difficult times in their playing days too and offered Beth some words of wisdom.

'Come back stronger,' they told her. 'It will be all the sweeter.'

*

Ten days later, Team GB began their Olympic dream. Their first match was played early in the morning

UK time, so Beth caught the first half before heading to pre-season training at Arsenal. Watching her teammates for club and country line up together in a strange kit somehow didn't feel real.

'It's like watching a fantasy football team,' Beth told Jordan in the gym.

'Would we feel worse if it they were wearing England shirts?' Jordan asked.

Probably, they decided.

It was so hard. Beth honestly wanted her friends to do well, but a small part of her wanted Hege to fail too.

A couple of days later, Phil called out of the blue. He was phoning to check in with Beth, but could tell she was ready to hear some home truths.

'Do you want to be Beth Mead who's happy eating fish and chips in Whitby, or do you want to be Beth Mead who's banging in goals at the big tournaments?' he asked her bluntly. She had the talent, now she had to make the most of it, he explained.

Beth listened calmly to every word. All around her people still believed in her, now she had to start believing in herself again.

In the end, Beth didn't miss out on a medal – Team GB went out in the quarter-finals. Ellen scored a hat-trick but it wasn't enough to stop Australia earning a 4–3 victory in extra time.

Beth's heart broke for Ellen, but otherwise she just felt numb. She was even glad that Team GB were out, though she never said so out loud. Now, she could try to move on and shake off the dark cloud that was hanging over her.

She would start by putting all her efforts into impressing Arsenal's new coach, Jonas Eidevall. She didn't want to be out in the cold at her club too.

*

That same month though, Beth took a call that saw her whole world come crashing down. She knew there was something wrong instantly when Mum's face flashed up on the screen. June looked drained, serious.

Mum hadn't wanted to tell Beth until she was sure, but the doctors had confirmed some sad news that day. Scans had shown that she had a horrible disease.

One that would need every ounce of energy and a course of brutal treatment to fight it. It was cancer.

Beth called Jonas next, still shaking. 'Go home to your family,' he told her. 'Nothing is more important.'

So Beth drove the 250 miles home to Hinderwell without stopping. Her stomach churned with a mix of shock, guilt and fear for the weeks and months ahead.

When she arrived, Beth melted into her mum's arms.

They sat for hours talking everything through together. The illness, the treatments she would need and what might happen in the future.

'If I'm going to fight this disease, then you need to fight for your place,' Mum told her daughter firmly. 'At Arsenal and England.'

Mum had already decided, Beth would return to London the next day and continue playing football. Beth begged to stay, but it made no difference, Mum had made her mind up.

And just like that, Beth felt the darkness that had cast a shadow over her since Hege's rejection begin to fade.

'I've got to stay positive and give Mum a reason to keep smiling,' she said, determined.

There would be no more sulking, no more looking back. The future was what mattered.

CHAPTER 12

A CLEAN SLATE

Beth was glad when the 2021–22 season finally
came around. It had been months since she'd played
a proper match. Jonas had helped her rediscover her
love of the game – he didn't see aggression, only
commitment.

'Keep doing what you do best,' he told her. 'Win
those fifty-fifty balls, beat those defenders. We need
you!'

He had been brilliant with Mum's illness too. And
she couldn't have wished for better teammates – they
all had her back. Chats over coffee, dog walks, hugs.
'Whatever you need,' they told her. Beth felt safe,
protected in an Arsenal bubble.

Then some good news at last – with Sarina
Wiegman now in charge of England, Beth was back in
the squad!

'Always an honour . . . can't wait to get back to it
with the Lionesses!' Beth updated her social media.
Now just two weeks to wait until camp!

When the day arrived at last, nerves began to
bubble in Beth as she headed to the team hotel at St
George's Park. Yes, she was back in the squad, but
there were no guarantees she would play. Would
Sarina like her? Would her infamous 'player report'
still count against her?

She needn't have worried – the new coach put her
at ease from their first conversation. 'You're a good
player,' Sarina reminded her. 'So go play with freedom,
enjoy your football.'

Beth asked about the player report.

'Some see aggression, I see passion,' Sarina said
plainly. 'Let's use that.'

Just like Jonas at Arsenal, Sarina was on Beth's
wavelength. Without her passion, Beth would be half
the player. It felt like an enormous weight had been

lifted from her shoulders.

As they talked further, Beth felt ready to open up – she had to tell Sarina about Mum. Beth explained that there might be tough days ahead, when she might need some time out or lose her cool.

Sarina listened and nodded. She got it straightaway. Someone she loved was suffering too.

'We'll be here for each other,' Sarina smiled. 'Players, staff . . . we'll be a family away from home.'

Their first training session together was a joy. The same joy she'd felt playing in Hinderwell, all those years ago. It flowed back through her body and straight to her feet, while the smile had returned to her face.

*

'We're going to play 4–3–3 against North Macedonia,' Sarina explained. 'Beth – you'll be on the right wing.'

Wow! Beth was back in the starting line-up for Sarina's debut as England boss! It was their first match on a road that would hopefully lead the Lionesses to the World Cup in Australia and New Zealand. Even with a few injuries and some new players to bed into the squad, Sarina expected her side to take all three points.

Beth beamed as she pulled on the gleaming white Lionesses shirt once again at St Mary's Stadium in Southampton. Running on to the pitch, she made sure to clap the fans in every corner of the ground.

England delivered for their new boss, and in style! Beth played the whole match, scoring in added time to seal an 8–0 victory.

The second match that camp went better still! This time, Beth started as a sub against minnows Luxembourg, but was in the thick of the action once on the pitch. In just half an hour, she created three fine assists for the team.

So the following month, Beth was gutted to learn she was benched again for the Northern Ireland game – at Wembley Stadium, no less.

'I need to see a little bit more from you, Beth,' Sarina had told her frankly before the match.

Beth had nodded at the time, but now sat stewing on the subs' bench.

Four assists and a goal in my last two matches.

What 'more' am I supposed to do?

Then her thoughts drifted to her mum and the promise she had made herself. She quickly snapped out of her sulk. If she did get the chance to go on, her feet would do the talking.

As expected, England took charge, hardly giving Northern Ireland a touch. But after an hour, the game was still goalless. Lauren Hemp and Alex Greenwood had hit the bar. Ellen and Leah had missed chances too.

Then a few minutes later, Sarina prepared a double substitution. Bethany England and Beth Mead were coming on. The two Bethanys!

This is it, thought Beth as she stepped on to the pristine Wembley pitch. *I'll show Sarina I'm more than just a bench-warmer!*

Soon after, a chance came her way. As the ball swung in from a corner, it bobbled towards her in the box. Beth stretched out a leg and produced an acrobatic half-volley on the turn. The keeper was completely stranded!

Goooooooooooooooaaaaaaaaaaaaalllllllllllll!

Beth had scored with her first touch.

Sarina smiled from the sidelines, as Wembley went wild.

Next, it was Bethany England's turn to get on the scoresheet: 2–0 with a tap-in.

'Talk about super subs!' the TV commentator raved. The Lionesses were roaring at last!

Three minutes later, Beth doubled her tally, firing home with a fierce right-foot volley. She was on a hat-trick now!

'Yes, Meado!' Ella Toone rushed to congratulate Beth.

And when the chance to grab her third popped up, Beth wasn't about to waste it. She slid home into the bottom corner with ease. *Boom!*

It had taken Beth just fourteen minutes to score her first England hat-trick, becoming the first woman to score three at Wembley. She had just written herself into the history books!

Maybe Sarina does know what she's doing, after all! Beth allowed herself a smile, as the coach flashed her a big thumbs-up.

Final score: 4–0. The match ball would be going home with Beth.

'To score a hat-trick for your country at Wembley . . . it's one of the proudest moments for me and my family,' Beth buzzed in her interview in the centre circle.

By now, the stadium was almost empty. The fans had flowed out into the night, on to trains and buses home. Beth surveyed the deserted stands, while still hugging the ball tightly. She imagined the scene the next summer, with every seat filled for the final of the Women's Euro. Close to 90,000 people could be cheering on the Lionesses if everything went their way.

'I've got to keep working hard,' the words came tumbling out. 'I've got to be a part of this squad.'

CHAPTER 13

THE BETH MEAD REVENGE TOUR

One week on, the draw was made for the Women's Euro, set to be played in ten stadiums up and down the country the following summer. The strongest teams were seeded into different pots, which meant that the Lionesses couldn't meet Netherlands, Germany or France until later in the tournament.

Instead, they were matched with two nations from their World Cup qualifying group – Austria and Northern Ireland – along with Norway.

At London Colney, Arsenal's Lionesses, Beth, Jordan, Leah and Lotte were watching the draw over breakfast.

'We'll take that,' said Jordan, saluting the TV screen with her protein shake.

'Definitely,' said Beth. 'We could have had Sweden or Spain in our group.'

'To be the best, we've got to beat the best!' said Leah wisely.

To the others, it seemed like Leah had always had an older head on her shoulders than her twenty-four years. The young defender had been so calm and positive since breaking into Arsenal's first team at just seventeen.

Sarina recognised these qualities in Leah too, trusting her with the captain's armband for England's recent matches while Steph was out injured. Steph had been a legendary leader over the years, but she was Mark Sampson's choice, and Phil's too. And nothing in football lasted forever.

So when Leah was unveiled as Sarina's permanent captain, Beth's heart burst with pride. She felt sure Leah would be brilliant.

'So proud 💚,' she wrote on social media.

Beth was proud of herself too. She had put her

Olympics pain behind her, and was playing some of her best football ever. Some fans had named Beth's return to form as the 'Beth Mead Revenge Tour'.

'This is just the start!' she promised.

Beth carried her amazing form into England's next matches – first at Sunderland's Stadium of Light, while their jaw-dropping 20–0 victory over Latvia was the Lionesses' biggest ever win. Beth bagged her second international hat-trick, alongside a hat-trick of assists.

The following spring saw Beth scoring four goals in a 10–0 thrashing of North Macedonia, and England winning the first Arnold Clark Cup. Playing under Sarina, Beth struck every shot with confidence and took on players with a self-belief she had never known before. She felt like she was walking on air.

Beth studied the stats since the Dutch coach had taken charge . . .

Eleven games.

Nine wins.

Two draws.

Zero defeats.

Two goals conceded.

Seventy-two goals scored! Thirteen of those by Beth!

England were building something special.

*

St George's Park, 15 June 2022

It was the morning of the Women's Euro squad announcement. In other words: D-Day. As the girls milled around the hotel at England's training base, the only person that was calm was Lucy.

'How can you be so laid back?' Beth asked.

Lucy had it all planned. First the Euros, then she was joining Barcelona, recent winners of the Champions League. Everyone else was full of nervous energy. Even Jill, who had been to tons of major tournaments with England, was feeling jittery.

'I can't tell whether it's nerves or the three coffees I've just drunk!' she joked.

'You're one hundred per cent going!' Beth promised.

One by one, the players were called in to see the boss.

Beth entered the room nervously. 'Last time this happened, I didn't make it,' she reminded Sarina about her unhappy Olympics experience.

'A different time, a different manager,' said Sarina plainly. But when she looked up, all the colour had drained from Beth's face. The coach cut to the chase. 'Congratulations,' said Sarina, smiling. 'You're in my squad.'

Beth breathed out a huge sigh of relief. 'Thank you!' she mouthed silently.

Sarina handed Beth a sticker of herself to stick in a football album that had been created specially to mark the occasion. Beth grinned. Her younger self would have loved collecting the stickers, but nothing like this had existed for women's football when she was growing up.

She raced back to her room to share the good news with her family.

'I'm going to the Euros!' Beth screamed down the phone.

'Of course you are, love!' her parents replied.

The tears came instantly. Not just Beth's, Mum and

Dad's too. All the hard work, the days and weeks apart while Mum was having her treatment had been worth it.

'We'll make this a summer to remember,' Beth promised, wiping away her happy tears.

*

Making the Euros squad wasn't the only big news in Beth's life that summer. Things were changing off the pitch too.

As a young woman, Beth had struggled with relationships. It had taken a long time to admit to herself and to her family that she was gay. When it finally clicked that you can't help who you fall in love with, Beth began to feel much happier in her own skin. Now she was proud to share pictures of the people she loved on social media, or talk about them in interviews.

Beth felt lucky. She knew that women's football was a safe space for players and fans, whatever their gender or whoever they chose to love. It was much tougher for her friends in men's football, where attitudes still had a long way to go to catch up with the real world. Sadly, there was no way a men's player could post a picture with a boyfriend without getting nasty comments.

When Beth and her Arsenal teammate Vivianne Miedema had grown close in recent months, it had caught them both by surprise. They had known each other for years now without any hint of a crush on either side. In fact, when Queen Viv first arrived at Arsenal and stole Beth's spot as striker, Beth didn't like her one bit!

Whoever said 'opposites attract' wasn't wrong: Beth was bubbly and outgoing, while Viv was quiet and serious. Beth had definitely helped to bring Viv out of her shell as they had spent more time together, while Viv helped keep Beth's feet on the ground.

The Arsenal fans were happy too. They had already nicknamed the couple 'Meadema', from their goalscoring feats on the pitch.

So when a final home friendly before the Euros was announced, it felt like fate. England would face reigning European champions Netherlands – Viv's team!

'We were destined to play you!' Beth joked to Viv.

No one expected a 5–1 scoreline, though! Beth scored twice on an electric night at Elland Road, Leeds. The Lionesses were peaking at just the right time – would any nation be able to stop them at the Euros?

Beth and Viv walked down the tunnel after the match with an arm around each other. Now the ninety minutes were up, they were no longer rivals.

'Sorry about the goals,' Beth apologised.

'Sorry *not sorry*, you mean,' Viv replied. 'I don't want to be on the same pitch as you again until Wembley!'

Wembley! Beth shivered. It was just days now until England would kick off the Euros. And in about six weeks' time, the new champions of Europe would be crowned at Wembley Stadium.

Excitement rippled through Beth's body. *Could England go all the way to the final? Maybe they would even play Netherlands?*

For the first time in a long time, Beth allowed herself to dream.

CHAPTER 14

TAKING ON EUROPE

England opened the Euros with a win over Austria at Old Trafford, where Beth's solo effort was enough to earn three points. A trip to Brighton on the south coast was next, but this time they faced tougher opposition. Norway had some brilliant players, not least Ada Hegerberg, the all-time top scorer of the Champions League.

No one could have predicted what happened next. Not the players. Not the press. Not even the fans. The Lionesses' demolition of Norway was a match that would go down in history.

Sarina trusted the same eleven to get the job done. Lucy, Ellen, Millie Bright – players with the big-game experience that counted. Beth started on the right again too. The opening minutes were nervy, tight, but after that, everything England did began to click.

Ellen won an early penalty, smashed home by Georgia Stanway. Then Beth flicked a ball into Lauren Hemp to make it 2–0 after fifteen minutes. The fans in the stands whooped and cheered loudly, but they would need to save their voices – more goals were yet to come! Next, Ellen burst into the box and unleashed a fantastic finish, before Lauren sent in a pinpoint cross for Beth to head home her first goal. Norway were crumbling!

They couldn't stop Beth as she danced through the defence to grab her second, nor Ellen at the far post who made it 6–0 before half-time.

'What is happening?' Ellen gasped.

Beth couldn't explain it, but every pass, cross or shot that she made was coming off. This was the stuff of dreams.

After fifty-seven minutes, Sarina made a triple substitution. Alessia Russo scored her first goal of the tournament, with Beth adding another before the final whistle. A hat-trick at the Euros! The Player of the Match was rightly hers.

Norway were utterly broken – their star striker Ada Hegerberg had hardly had a kick.

England 8 Norway 0, it finished. The biggest score ever in a Women's Euros match, this was one for the history books! The Lionesses had played the perfect game and made it look like a kickabout in the park.

'I can't put it into words,' Beth told the BBC. 'It's an incredible feeling to feel how I do right now.'

Back in the dressing room, Beth couldn't stop beaming. Sarina had chosen the best teammates Beth could wish for – amazing role models for any little girl growing up. Her heart burst with both pride and love for these Lionesses. They were enjoying every moment of their journey together.

The tournament rolled on with another goal-fest, this time against neighbours Northern Ireland. Beth scored for the third match in a row, her fifth goal in total. The girl from Yorkshire was fast becoming the toast of Europe!

*

Next, a return to Brighton beckoned, where Spain would be England's opponents. Even without their injured star Alexia Putellas, La Roja had players all over the pitch who could cause damage. A massive test lay ahead.

Indeed, it was Spain who started stronger, dominating the first half hour. Then against the run of play, Ellen put the ball in the back of the net, but offside!

'Let's keep our heads up!' Beth rallied.

In the fifty-fourth minute, Spain's Esther González broke the deadlock, stroking the ball past Mary Earps, as a stunned silence swept around the ground.

Nooooo! Beth's heart sank. The Lionesses had to score, or their Euros dream would be over.

Minutes later, the board went up. Beth and Ellen had seen their last action for the night and maybe even the tournament. It was a brave call from Sarina – taking off the Euros' top goalscorer and the leading Lionesses goalscorer of all time. The players on the pitch, though, still believed. Beth felt positive too – there were more goals in this game.

Next Lauren went down in the box under a clumsy challenge, but to the crowd's astonishment a free kick was given against England. No penalty! The game rumbled on with Spain looking more likely to score again than allow England an equaliser. With eighty-two minutes gone, England had to gamble. Millie was pushed up front as an extra striker.

Then it came. Alessia nodded down Lauren's whipped-in cross, straight into the path of substitute Ella Toone who stuck out a boot to volley home from five yards.

As extra time loomed, England began to look calmer, more composed. Spain were on the back foot and looking rattled. Then, the winning goal came. Georgia Stanway drove from midfield towards the box. With the Spain defenders backing off, Georgia picked her spot and slammed the ball past Sandra Paños.

Goooooaaaaallll!

The cheers almost blew the roof off the stadium, as choruses of 'It's Coming Home' rang out around the ground for the first time that night. Too soon? Beth kept everything crossed that it wasn't.

After that, any Spanish attack found a dead end. England were magnificent! They blocked every ball and used every trick in the book to wind down the seconds.

Then finally, after 120 minutes and four more minutes of added time, England were semi-finalists!

Even Sarina, usually so cool and calm, pumped both fists with emotion. What a night! The Lionesses had faced a setback and come through it with flying colours. Now they could catch their breath before a date with Sweden in Sheffield.

*

Thankfully, the semi-final at Bramall Lane was more straightforward – some of the fans had no nails left to bite! After a couple of early scares, England scored first when Lucy collected the ball on the wing and blasted it back into the box towards Beth. With her back to goal, the Arsenal winger controlled the ball and swivelled her shot goalwards past the diving Hedwig Lindahl. An unbelievable strike! The crowd thought so too!

After that, England took the game by the scruff of

the neck, creating chance after chance against the Olympic silver medallists. Early in the second half, Beth turned provider for Lucy, who buried her header. 2–0.

The next strike was so good it won Goal of the Tournament! Alessia's first shot from close range was blocked, but she wasn't giving up. With her back to goal in a crowded box, she went to backheel the ball. Through a defender's legs it rolled, then straight between the keeper's, too!

'That is absolutely sensational!' roared the commentator.

Beth could barely believe what she had just seen. 'Are you actually joking?' she gasped, before leaping into Alessia's arms.

And when Fran's delicious chip from outside the box beat Lindahl, England's place at Wembley was sealed.

At the final whistle, the entire squad sang 'Sweet Caroline' together. The good times had never felt so good!

CHAPTER 15

THE FINAL SHOWDOWN

31 July 2022, Wembley Stadium, London
Women's Euro 2022 final – England vs Germany

Beth stood in the Wembley tunnel, thoughts racing through her mind. The last time she had been in the famous stadium was as a fan, cheering on England's Three Lions in their own Euro final. All the while feeling miserable that she wasn't where she should have been – at the Olympics.

Now though, England's Lionesses had made it to their own final – the game of their lives! Just fifteen minutes remained until kick-off.

This is it. All the training sessions, the work in the

gym, the warm-up matches and the team talks, then winning all five matches on their way to the final – everything they had worked so hard for had led them to this moment. Now, only Germany stood between England and the Women's Euro trophy.

On paper, Germany looked almost unbeatable – the eight-time winners of the trophy had won all their matches so far too. Only France had managed to beat their defence all tournament and even that had been a lucky own goal. England did have one advantage though – most of the record-breaking 87,192 fans in the crowd would be on their side, hoping to roar them to victory as European Champions for the first time.

Sarina had named the same starting eleven for each match so far, and was sticking with her strongest line-up for the final. Playing on the wing, Beth had been on fire all tournament and was level on six goals with Germany's captain Alex Popp. If neither player scored again, Beth would win the Golden Boot trophy as she had more assists. Popp though was a menace – England's defenders had a massive job ahead of them to keep her quiet.

'Who will come out on top in the battle for the Golden Boot?' read the newspaper articles.

Beth wasn't worried about that. Her only goal was for England to win – it meant everything to her. Anything else would be a bonus.

Then, soon after the team photos, Germany made a last-minute change. A tearful Popp had to pull out injured. She couldn't even make the bench. Now only Alessia could challenge Beth for the Golden Boot.

To the crowd's delight, England made a bright start, with Beth involved in England's best moves. But by half-time, the game had become scrappy. Ellen had come the closest to scoring but saw her shot sail just over the bar. Would England rue their missed chances?

Early in the second half, German midfielder Lina Magull fired a warning shot wide of the post. Germany were turning up the heat, while England's nerves were beginning to fray. At fifty-five minutes, Sarina brought on fresh legs. On came Ella and Alessia. Could the fearless Manchester United duo put their stamp on the game?

Close to the hour mark, Lucy fed a ball to Beth, who tangled with Marina Hegering. Both players felt the pain, but Beth came off worse. Lucy rushed over to help, massaging Beth's calf with a worried look. When that didn't work, Beth hobbled to the sidelines for more treatment.

Seconds later, Germany were caught off guard. Keira found Ella with a defence-splitting pass to put her through on goal. The Germany defenders couldn't catch her; now all Ella had to do was to beat the keeper. England's super sub somehow kept her cool and scooped the ball up and over Merle Frohms. What a finish! England were in front!

'The goalscorer for England, Number 20, ELLA TOOOOOOONE!' the stadium announcer boomed as the crowd exploded.

Incredible! Beth was still receiving treatment when she felt an urge to run back on to the pitch to celebrate with Ella. The physio and her leg told her otherwise. 'Yes, Tooney!' she screamed.

It pained her to say it, but Beth had given all she could. She had run off dead legs before, but this one had her beaten. 'Bring Chloe on,' she told Sarina. 'We can use her energy.'

So Beth headed to the bench to heartfelt cheers from the fans, as Chloe Kelly replaced her.

The game carried on at a frantic pace. Germany hit the bar before scoring a well-worked goal in the seventy-ninth minute.

'Keep going, girls,' said Leah.

And they did until the ref blew. Extra time!

If anyone can do this, it's us – it's England – Beth was convinced. Even if it came down to a penalty shoot-out.

Thankfully the fans were spared penalties, as Chloe poked home from a corner with ten minutes of extra time left. It was a scrappy strike from five yards out, but to Beth it was the most magnificent goal that England had ever scored!

GOOOOOAAAAAAAAALLLLLLLLLL! The sub stripped off her shirt and began swinging it around her head like a lasso.

Now England had the lead again, it was theirs for keeps. After the goal, they barely gave Germany a touch of the ball.

'We've got this, girls!' Beth screamed. She was kicking every ball from the bench!

Then at last the ref raised her whistle to her mouth and blew. Full-time.

ENGLAND HAD DONE IT! THEY WERE CHAMPIONS OF EUROPE!!!!

Beth's dead leg suddenly vanished, as she hurled herself into a huddle of Lionesses. The scenes that followed were like nothing the players had ever experienced before. The tears, the hugs, the singing and dancing – these were moments too special to ever forget. Beth found Alex Popp for a hug and a handshake too.

Then an official pulled Beth aside. Her trophies were ready and waiting to be claimed – not only had her team won the Euros, Beth had been named the Player of the Tournament and bagged the Golden Boot as well!

Mum, Dad and Ben Mead cheered louder than anyone in the ground. As Beth made her way behind the advertising hoardings to find them, the tears wouldn't stop. The family came together in an emotional embrace.

'We're going to need a bigger trophy cabinet!' said Mum.

Still in her kit, Beth headed to a press conference next.

'A history-maker, a trailblazer, an icon,' the journalist crowned her. How did that make her feel?

Beth smiled. It felt so strange for someone to be using those words to describe her. The journalist was right, though; Beth and the Lionesses had just made history – they had become the first England team to win a trophy in fifty-six years!

'I'm just Beth Mead, that's me,' she replied humbly. 'I play football. It's a dream come true to be doing what I'm doing.'

From the age of six, football had been the love of her life. Some things would never change.

CHAPTER 16

THE CELEBRATIONS CONTINUE

As sunlight streamed in through the half-closed curtains of her hotel room the next morning, Beth rolled over in bed and rubbed her eyes. *What time was it anyway?* She reached for her phone.

About a thousand notifications and messages flashed up on the screen. Everyone wanted to congratulate Europe's new golden girl! They would have to wait for a reply for now.

Beth had only been asleep for about two hours, after the party had slipped well into the next morning. Better than nothing! she told herself, wondering whether some of the girls had even been to bed at all.

Coffee would have to fuel her today, as the team

were due to greet the fans that lunchtime at a special celebration in Trafalgar Square.

When the team boarded the coach, Beth quickly felt like the odd one out. Almost all of her teammates were wearing white T-shirts with the word 'HOME' emblazoned in red, after the Lionesses had finally brought football home.

'Looks like we missed the memo!' Beth joked to Sarina, comparing her own grey training top with that of the coach's.

Sarina shrugged with a twinkle in her eye.

Beth braced herself to be called the teacher's pet. The others were always teasing her for speaking Dutch to the boss – little phrases she'd picked from hanging out with Arsenal's Dutch players.

For the hour-long journey into town, the music blared loudly, with the whole squad singing along. Leah knew exactly what to put on the playlist to keep the party vibes going!

As they neared their destination, cars and vans beeped loudly. The bus was black and ordinary looking, but the secret had somehow leaked out – the

Lionesses were on board! Traffic ground to a standstill as everyone stopped to welcome the new European Champions.

Beth and her teammates were used to fans, but this was a whole new level. It felt like they had gone from footballers to film stars overnight!

'Beep your horn back!' Beth begged the driver. The team wanted to show just how much they appreciated everyone's support.

A stage in front of Nelson's Column looked out towards Trafalgar Square's two famous fountains. About 7,000 fans had gathered to greet the new champions in sweltering temperatures.

On the front row were June, Richard and Ben Mead. Beth waved, before slinking to the back of the stage. She was more than was happy for others to take centre-stage off the pitch.

Then it was over to Alex Scott, once an England and Arsenal player herself, to introduce a video reminding the crowd of exactly how the famous trophy had been won. A sea of St George flags waved wildly in appreciation.

Interviews followed, with Sarina and Leah, and then Ella and Chloe, the goalscorers from the final. Next, Alex scanned the stage for Beth, who reluctantly stepped forwards.

'Meado! Meado!' her teammates on the stage all chanted.

Beth suddenly felt both emotional and hoarse at once. *Should I have prepared a speech? Too late now!*

When Alex reminded Beth that she was the Player of the Tournament, it still didn't feel real. Would it ever sink in? Next the conversation took a different tack. 'You got left out, you came back, and you've shown the world what you were capable of . . .' Alex began.

Beth's thoughts quickly flicked to the previous summer. The pain of missing out on the Olympics had at last faded away. Playing out of her skin to help win the Euros with her family by her side – these were the memories that mattered.

'Yeah, sometimes football sucks, but I worked hard and feel so lucky to be part of this team,' Beth replied. 'I'm just so happy to be here.'

Just as she always did, Beth spoke from the heart.

Interview over, she breathed a sigh of relief. It was time to bring out the trophy!

Leah raised the elegant glass trophy once more, as fireworks blazed behind the stage and silvery ticker tape rained down. Then players and staff linked arms for what felt like the one thousandth 'Sweet Caroline' of the summer. It would be a Lionesses anthem forever now!

The party was in full swing when Jill Scott grabbed the mic and pretended to interview the trophy, which was now wearing its own bucket hat. Then it was time for Rachel Daly to transform from footballer to rock diva and lead another sing-along. Rach was never shy on their team karaoke nights, but this was next level. Her performance of 'River Deep, Mountain High' to thousands rocked!

I could never do that in a million years! Beth blushed.

What an amazing party! She felt so proud to be a part of this squad, making memories together that they would hold tight for the rest of their lives.

*

It was on the coach home that Lotte had a brainwave. Now that the Lionesses were European Champions, they had a platform to help change the game. There was still so much work to be done to give girls the same opportunities as boys to play football.

'We'll use our voice and write a public letter demanding that all girls are allowed to play football at school,' Lotte suggested.

Growing up, hardly any of the Lionesses had got to play football in PE lessons, unlike most boys their age. Girls had had to set up their own teams, often travelling miles to play. Little had changed since.

'Brilliant idea,' said Beth. 'We have to do this.'

'There's so much we can achieve together,' added Leah.

The Lionesses got off the coach feeling fired up about the future. And for the first time in weeks, they were now officially off duty!

As they said their goodbyes, hunger pangs suddenly hit.

'I need food – and fast,' Beth said to Leah. 'Think we've we earned a cheeky Big Mac?' Leah didn't need asking twice!

When their car pulled into the drive-through restaurant, the servers' jaws nearly hit the floor – they could never have imagined serving a couple of Lionesses that day.

'Posting a photo of us eating junk food was probably not your best idea,' Beth joked, as she and Leah flipped open their burger boxes.

'Nah, Sarina doesn't do social media . . .' Leah said, munching on her burger. 'Does she?'

They hoped they would be forgiven, just this once.

Lotte set to work on the letter the next day. The United Kingdom was preparing to vote in a new prime minister, so the team addressed the letter to Liz Truss and Rishi Sunak, the politicians hoping to become the country's next leader. All twenty-three players signed it, united in their message.

Their message spread quickly on social media, gaining support far and wide. At last, girls' sport was being taken seriously.

CHAPTER 17

BACK TO THE GRIND

Beth felt like her feet hadn't touched the ground since that amazing day at Wembley. There were photoshoots, interviews, TV appearances – everyone wanted to get to know Europe's new golden girl. It was exhausting!

So when the chance came up to escape the media glare, Beth grabbed her passport and headed to Greece with Viv. A week to unwind was just what they needed.

Even a thousand miles from home though, British tourists stopped Beth for her autograph, or to tell her how proud they were of her and the team. Football fever had gripped the whole nation – the Lionesses were heroes!

One evening when the pair came to pay for dinner,

they discovered that a family had already settled the bill without a word. What an unexpected treat!

Beth wondered what it would be like when she landed back in England. Would the excitement have died down, or had the Lionesses changed the game for good?

*

On their return, it was back to training with Arsenal ahead of the new season. A heroes' welcome awaited Beth, Leah and Lotte at the Gunners' London Colney base. Both the men's and women's squads, along with all the staff, formed an enormous guard of honour to congratulate the three Lionesses.

Everyone wanted a peek at their gleaming Euros medals afterwards. Beth's had a small dint where she'd dropped hers – she wasn't quite sure when – while Leah's showed some tiny marks too.

'Why did no one tell me you're supposed to *pretend* to bite it?' the England skipper giggled.

Only Lotte's medal was still pristine!

There were big hugs from Bakayo Saka and Aaron Ramsdale, who had been a penalty or two away from winning their own Euro medals the summer before. The men's coach Mikel Arteta congratulated Beth on all her trophies too.

Beth was about to begin her sixth full season with Arsenal, and her bond with the club had never been stronger. It was more like being part of a big family than a football club. She had come such a long way from the shy, homesick girl that had first moved to London.

Even though it felt to Beth like the Euros had only just ended, the new Women's Super League season was right around the corner. There were old rivalries to resume, as well as new battles to fight. It was time to get back to the grind.

Since becoming a Gunner, Beth had won a league title and the League Cup, before a trophy drought that had lasted for four seasons. Their 2021–22 campaign had seen Arsenal finish second by a single point as London rivals Chelsea were crowned champions again. So close!

Beth hated losing – it didn't suit her! *This season will be different*, she vowed to herself. *It has to be.*

Wherever she was, on the pitch or in the gym, her mum was always in her thoughts.

By now, Mum's illness was getting worse. Throughout those difficult weeks, Beth never heard her mum complain and she never gave up. Instead, she inspired Beth to keep working hard, even on the days when she wanted to give it all up and run home to Hinderwell.

The best way I can make Mum proud is on a football pitch, she repeated to herself. I've got to keep going, one day at a time.

Arsenal's opening league match was a home tie against Hope Powell's Brighton. It felt so good to be back in Arsenal colours, one freezing Friday evening in September. While a sell-out crowd had crammed into every stand at Meadow Park, there should have been a party atmosphere. Instead, an air of sadness hung around the ground. As the sun set, the teams stood together for a minute's silence to remember Her Majesty the Queen, who had passed away earlier in the month.

The game got off to a dramatic start when – *RED*

CARD! – Brighton's Emma Kullberg was sent off after only six minutes of play. The Seagulls were in for a long night! Despite being a player down, Brighton defended courageously – blocking, tackling, heading and clearing every ball that Arsenal launched into their box. It took half an hour to break them down, when Kim finished well from a Caitlin Foord cut-back. 1–0.

Truth be told, Arsenal's attackers had looked a little rusty in the first half. Jonas wanted more from his team. More urgency. More accuracy too.

After the break, Arsenal came out stronger. Beth received the ball and quickly fed in Stina Blackstenius. The Swedish striker blasted a fine shot into the top corner. Next, Beth added her own name to the scoresheet after Viv stroked the ball into her path for a first-time finish.

'This is more like it!' Jonas clapped from the sidelines.

Late in the game, Beth made it four. The Number 9 had all the time in the world to control the ball and pick her spot. Arsenal were cruising!

What a night, under the lights! Beth had carried over her brilliant form from the Euros straight into the new season – she was simply unstoppable! She hoped her hot streak would last the whole season, or at least until the North London derby.

CHAPTER 18

EMIRATES EXPECTS

Since Tottenham had been promoted to the Women's Super League, their matches with Arsenal had always been exciting contests. The home and away games were the first matches that players and fans alike looked for when the fixture lists came out before the start of each season. Whoever won the North London derby would earn the bragging rights too!

Beth thought back to the first time the two teams had met in the WSL in 2019. What an incredible occasion! Arsenal had beaten Spurs at their sparkly new Tottenham Hotspur Stadium, in front of a record crowd – goals from Kim and Viv crowning a classy display from the away side.

Until that season, the women's teams could only dream of playing at the huge stadiums where the men played, but slowly the tide was turning. More than 38,000 fans had come to watch that game, setting a new record for a WSL match. After the World Cup in France though, the appetite for watching women's football had been steadily growing.

'We were champions back when we played Spurs in 2019,' Viv reminded Beth.

'And you were top scorer that season too,' Beth replied.

Now they had more trophies with Arsenal in their sights.

In September 2022, Arsenal and Spurs met again, this time at Emirates Stadium. The Gunners were the stronger side on paper and the fans expected them to win, but Beth knew that in football anything could happen. Nothing less than a win would do.

This time, over 47,000 fans were expected – more than ten times the number that packed into their usual ground, Meadow Park in Boreham Wood. The record attendance belonging to Spurs was about to be smashed to pieces!

Out on the pitch, Jonas kept his team talk brief. 'It's our job to repay these fantastic supporters with a big performance,' he told his huddle of players. 'So go show everyone what we can do!'

They each placed a hand in the middle of the circle. 'Let's do this, girls,' said Kim, Arsenal's captain. 'Let's win the North London derby!'

The Gunners burst into action from the first whistle, with Beth firing an early shot on target. Finding herself unmarked in the box, her shot deflected off a defender and out for a corner. Close.

'Keep your head up, Bethy,' said Kim. 'You'll get the next one.'

And she did. On Arsenal's next attack, Kim won a tackle by the halfway line and played a beautiful through ball to Beth. Beth passed to the far post, but it bounced off a defender straight back into her path. The chance opened up on her right foot and Beth bent her shot around the keeper. *Goooaaalll!*

Just five minutes had been played.

Emirates Stadium erupted, as chants of 'MEADO!

MEADO!' echoed around the ground.

'The fans' favourite and England hero can do no wrong right now!' the TV commentator blared.

Beth's goal had given Arsenal the confidence to turn on the style, as they started a beautiful display of one-touch passing. The Tottenham players couldn't win the ball back, no matter how hard they tried. Kim hit the side netting next, before Aussie attacker Caitlin Foord glanced a header just wide. Spurs were hanging on at 1–0, but for how much longer?

Then with a minute to go before half-time, Viv doubled Arsenal's lead. She loved scoring against rivals Tottenham! After Caitlin pressured the defender into making a mistake outside the Spurs box, the ball fell kindly to Arsenal's Number 11. Viv easily slotted home into the corner of the net. What a gift!

As usual, there was barely a flicker of celebration on Viv's face.

'About time you scored!' Beth said jokingly. Like it or not, Viv was Arsenal's goal machine!

The second half began much like the first – the visitors just couldn't cope with Arsenal's attackers. At fifty-four minutes, the Gunners scored again. Their Brazilian centre-back, Rafaelle, rose highest to meet Beth's corner and looped a strong header past the keeper. No one was saving that!

But Arsenal weren't about to take their foot off the gas. This crowd had come to be entertained! There was plenty of time for Viv to flick home another header and make it four. Game over.

With the three points in the bag, Jonas made some subs. Off went Viv and Caitlin, with Beth making way for new signing Lina Hurtig.

As she made her exit from the pitch, Beth was greeted with a standing ovation from the Emirates faithful. It seemed like every single fan was on their feet – men, women, girls and boys – all clapping wildly and chanting her name.

It felt incredible. In her five years at Arsenal, she couldn't remember ever having been given such an amazing reception before.

Beth clapped her hands above her head, drinking in every moment, goosebumps bristling on her arms. *One day we'll play in front of huge crowds like these every week,* she told herself.

The match finished 4–0 and the crowd roared again. North London was RED!

Beth was keen to thank the fans. They had such a special place in her heart. 'They give us such an energy. Hopefully this is just the beginning,' she told the TV cameras.

Back in the dressing room, the celebrations began to flow. While the singing and dancing grew louder around her, Beth sat motionless on the long bench, still dressed in full kit and boots.

Her mum, now too poorly to travel to matches, had messaged Beth as soon as the final whistle had blown. 'I'm so proud of you! x,' the text said.

Beth read the message over and over, as guilt trickled through her. She hated being so far away when all the time Mum was getting sicker and sicker. Meanwhile, Beth got to carry on playing the game she loved.

Kim came over and handed Beth a drinks bottle. 'Well done today,' she said, putting a hand on Beth's shoulder. 'You made the difference . . . you always do.'

CHAPTER 19

RETURN TO WEMBLEY

With World Cup qualification already sealed, next up for the Lionesses was a friendly match at Wembley Stadium in October 2022. Just how friendly a contest it would be remained to be seen. Opponents didn't come much bigger than the four-time world champions, the United States of America.

The last time the two teams had met was three years earlier in France. So much had changed since Alex Morgan had broken England hearts. Fans were desperate to see who would come out on top – would it be the world champions of 2019 or the newly crowned champions of Europe?

The Lionesses were excited to be back at Wembley,

for the first time since that historic July final. Since the summer though, Ellen had retired, Jill too. Now there was space in the squad for the next generation of players to make their name.

By now, Beth had learned to never take her place for granted – and it would be almost impossible to keep up the sensational form she had shown at the Euros. Competition was fierce too: Chloe Kelly, Lauren Hemp and now Lauren James were all strong players who could catch Sarina's eye.

The match against the USA had sold out in record time – all the tickets had been snapped up in a day or two, setting the stage for a fantastic homecoming. Wembley Walk had been decorated with banners of each player from England's championship-winning squad, while the famous Wembley arch was lit up in rainbow colours. The first banners to greet fans from the tube were of Jill and Ellen, while Beth's portrait was flanked either side by those of Georgia Stanway and Alex Greenwood. Every player a hero.

Inside the stadium, the atmosphere was electric. Even Lucy Bronze, on her way to one hundred caps, had never heard noise like it. Incredible!

Before the match, England's original team of Lionesses from 1972 were honoured with official caps. Attitudes had been very different back then, with women unfairly banned from playing football for fifty years in England, and in other countries too. The women's game had been playing catch-up ever since.

England's opponents, USA, were not quite at full strength, but could still boast.

World Cup winners Megan Rapinoe, Lindsey Horan, Rose Lavelle and keeper Alyssa Naeher in their starting line-up. More than enough talent to put the fear into most teams!

Meanwhile, the Lionesses were without their captain – Leah Williamson was nursing a hamstring injury, while young striker Alessia Russo was also out injured. This would be as big a test as any that England had faced under Sarina Wiegman, and it was up to the rest of the team to step up.

Lose tonight, and their twenty-two-match unbeaten run would be over.

An action-packed first half had the crowd in full

voice. Beth had an early chance when Georgia coolly backheeled the ball into her path on the edge of the box. The Arsenal forward unleashed her shot, but it flew straight into the arms of Alyssa Naeher.

It was England who did strike first, as early as the twelfth minute. Lucy spotted Beth's clever run, who then sent a smart cross into the box. When the USA defender got her legs in a tangle, the ball bobbled for Lauren Hemp to steal in and finish.

'England have taken the lead with the goal all about the run of Beth Mead!' said the commentator.

The camera panned to Leah in the stands, cheering on her teammates.

Just before the half-hour mark, though, USA equalised with a superb strike from Sophia Smith, after Georgia Stanway was bustled off the ball. The young American would be one to watch at the World Cup.

Shortly after, Lucy won a penalty after bravely putting her head on the end of an American boot to win the ball. Her middle name wasn't 'Tough' for nothing! No red card was given by the ref, but VAR awarded the spot-kick. Georgia made amends for her earlier error by expertly rolling the ball home. England were back in front.

Then, when Trinity Rodman scored for USA next, VAR saved the day again. Offside! The goal was chalked off by the tightest of margins.

The second half continued in a frenzy. It was end to end! Lucy skimmed the side netting, while a rocketing shot from Georgia whistled past the post. Megan and Trinity shot wide for USA too.

Then, disaster! When Rose Lavelle's effort was blocked by Lauren Hemp in the box, the ref pointed to the spot. The ball was judged to have hit Lauren's arm. But when the ref checked the monitors, the video clearly showed that the ball had struck her on the bottom. No penalty!

The crowd breathed out an enormous sigh of relief.

Despite some nervy moments, England saw out the game. They had survived to keep their unbeaten streak alive!

'What a ninety minutes!' Beth panted, as the Lionesses jogged down the tunnel.

'Player of the match has got to go to VAR!' laughed Lauren.

The USA coach Vlatko Andonovski was full of praise for England after the match.

'They have an incredible squad. I wouldn't mind facing them again in the final!'

He was talking about the World Cup final, of course, due to be decided the following summer. Just like always, Sarina tried not to look too far ahead. It was important to keep the players' feet on the ground. The final in Sydney was still over ten months away, and while England were making good progress, experience told her that anything could happen between now and then.

CHAPTER 20

THE BALLON D'OR

The *Ballon d'Or* or 'Golden Football' was a prestigious trophy awarded each year to the world's best footballer. A string of famous names had won the award in the men's game over the decades, but the first women's version had only been awarded in 2018. Ada Hegerberg, of Norway and Lyon, had won the very first *Ballon d'Or Féminin*.

While most footballers agreed they would rather win a team trophy over an individual award any day, winning the famous *Ballon d'Or* remained a dream for any player. The huge gold trophy would look good on any player's mantelpiece!

The Arsenal girls were sitting by the swimming pool

at London Colney the day the nominations were due out. A shortlist of twenty of the best female footballers would be announced.

Just three Lionesses had been nominated in previous years: Lucy Bronze, Fran Kirby and Ellen White, with Lucy coming the closest to winning when she finished as runner-up to Megan Rapinoe after her epic performances at the 2019 World Cup.

So when Beth found out she had been nominated following England's success at the Euros, she was staggered. She knew something big had happened when her phone started buzzing with what felt like a thousand notifications!

And there she was, tagged in a post on the official *Ballon d'Or* Twitter account: Beth Mead, Arsenal, forward, in the running for the 2022 *Ballon d'Or Féminin*. Incredible!

And it wasn't only Beth, her fellow Lionesses Lucy and Millie had earned nominations too.

'Viv,' said Beth excitedly, scrolling on her phone. 'You've made the list too!'

Viv shrugged. For the Dutch forward, the novelty

had worn off a little. This was the third time she'd been up for the award.

'You stand a much better chance of winning than me – you're a European Champion!' Viv reminded Beth.

Immediately, Beth's thoughts turned to her family. *The news can't have travelled that fast, or they would have called!* As they had done when she'd won all her other medals . It was something that Beth did to try to help pay back her parents. All those hours spent driving their daughter up and down the country for training and matches – she could never have become a professional footballer without them.

Two months later, Beth and Viv found themselves travelling in style to the awards ceremony . . . on a private jet! Bukayo Saka from Arsenal's men's squad was joining them on the short flight to Paris. He was up for the Kopa Trophy, a special award for young players.

The three posed for a photo in the plush leather seats.

'You're probably used to this,' Viv teased Bukayo. Male footballers were much more pampered than the women.

'Nah, it's my first time too,' he replied excitedly. He was as excited to be there as the girls!

They put on their seatbelts, ready for take-off.

'What do you reckon then?' Bukayo asked Beth. 'You going to win?'

'I doubt it,' smiled Beth. 'Alexia is a baller!'

Alexia Putellas, Spain and Barcelona's midfield ace, was the current holder of the *Ballon d'Or Féminin*. She was tipped to win the title for the second time despite suffering a bad knee injury on the eve of the Euros.

A. C. L. The letters stood for anterior cruciate ligament and were the three letters that no professional footballer wanted to hear. The dreaded knee injury meant surgery and usually more than nine months out of the game. Alexia's tournament had ended before a game had even kicked off.

Would England still have beaten Spain in their Euros quarter-final with Alexia in the team? Beth liked to think so. But when it came to the *Ballon d'Or*, Beth felt less confident about her own chances of winning. Journalists from all over the world would all have had to agree that Beth had played better that year than

Alexia. Win or lose though, Beth was thrilled to even be mentioned in the same breath as the best players on the planet.

That night, Beth and Viv arrived at the Théâtre du Châtelet for the fancy ceremony, both dressed in sleek black cocktail gowns. Rows of photographers had gathered to snap the stars of world football, including French heroes Kylian Mbappé and Karim Benzema.

'Please don't let me fall over in these heels!' Beth whispered to Viv, as they stepped carefully out of their car on to the red carpet.

Behind them, Alexia Putellas arrived, in a gown that sparkled from head to toe. 'She's definitely dressed to win!' Beth whispered to Viv.

And sure enough, Alexia kept her crown as football's golden girl.

Beth clapped as loudly as anyone. Alexia was a queen! It was heartbreaking that she had had to miss the Euros. Beth knew what it was like to miss a tournament, but never because of such a terrible injury. She could only imagine the pain.

CHAPTER 21

SERIOUS SETBACKS

A month on from Paris, Arsenal were back in action at Emirates Stadium. The players were excited for the league to get started again after the November international break.

Like Arsenal, visitors Manchester United had started the season strongly, and could go level on points with the Gunners at the top of the league if they won.

Beth was feeling sharp before the match under the lights that evening. The stadium where the men played suited her game – in her six appearances there, she'd scored four times and made two assists. And with a crowd of 40,000 fans, the stage was set for a memorable match.

'We've got a great record against this team,' Jonas finished his team talk. 'Let's keep it going and give the fans something to sing about.'

It wouldn't be plain sailing though; five Lionesses were named in Man United's starting line-up! Friendships would have to be put on hold until the final whistle had blown.

And sure enough, it was a Lioness who scored first. When Arsenal's keeper Manuela Zinsberger flapped unsuccessfully a cross, Ella Toone easily side-footed the ball into the gaping net. 0–1! Man United were in front.

It stayed that way until just after the break, when Frida Maanum put Arsenal back on level terms, helped by a lucky deflection. A brilliant volley from Laura Wienroither followed and the lead swung to Arsenal. What a game!

With just five minutes to go, Man United's Millie Turner headed home for 2–2, before Alessia Russo grabbed the winner in added time. Arsenal 2–3 Manchester United!

Losing their unbeaten run would have been bad enough for Arsenal, but something worse still was about to happen. There were just seconds left on the clock when Beth went in for a tackle. There wasn't much contact with the Man United player, but Beth fell awkwardly, twisting her knee.

She gingerly got to her feet again, but could feel tears prick her eyes. Something felt very wrong.

When the whistle blew, Jordan Nobbs, Arsenal's captain on the day, ran over and put an arm around her friend.

'This feels bad, Jords,' Beth said in a hushed voice.

If anyone knew about bad injuries, it was Jordan. She'd missed a World Cup and the Euros due to her own injury problems.

'Let's wait and see,' said Jordan, trying to stay positive.

Waiting was all Beth could do. She wouldn't know for sure how serious the injury was until the swelling had gone down.

A few days later, Beth lay on the doctor's couch. She had already decided that however bad the news that day, she was ready to do whatever it took to heal her knee. She stared at the scans glowing on the lightbox and waited nervously for the verdict.

'I'm afraid you've torn your anterior cruciate ligament,' the doctor told her.

Noooooooooooo! Beth understood straightaway. An ACL injury – the same as Alexia had suffered. It meant that her season with Arsenal was over. Recovering in time to play at the World Cup would need a superhuman effort too. It would be a race against time to be fit.

The very next month, Viv was stretchered off in tears at Arsenal's Champions League game against Lyon. As fate would have it, it was later revealed to be the same serious injury as Beth's. Viv, though, was less optimistic about her own chances of making the Netherlands World Cup squad. She had even less time to recover.

Both players had operations to fix their knees but would need crutches for the next few weeks.

'It's painful now, but we'll come back stronger,' Beth promised Viv.

That night, Beth lay awake, alone with her thoughts. She wished she knew what the universe was trying to tell her. Only a few weeks ago she'd felt like she was walking on air. Now her whole world was beginning to crumble around her. It was more than just the highs and lows of football too – over the past few months, tears had come almost daily.

Their family had been told that Mum's cancer had spread, and as the weeks had got colder, she had grown weaker and weaker. The news had hit Beth like a truck, she had never cried so much in her life.

Mum couldn't get to games any more, but her face still lit up watching every goal that Beth scored on TV. She would smile too at every mention of her daughter, superstar footballer Beth Mead, in the match reports that Dad read out loud.

The doctors couldn't say for sure how long June had left, but she had accepted that there was no coming back from this terrible disease. The damage was too great. What little time she was given would be spent surrounded by her family and friends, the people that loved her the most.

Beth tried to carry on as best as she could too. Her injury, now Viv's injury, and Mum's diagnosis – it was a truly horrible hat-trick. No one would have blamed Beth if she'd packed in football right there and then. But along with her family, football had always been Beth's first love. She was in this for better or worse.

Beth thought back to her days in the academies. Mum had worked so hard, taking on two jobs to afford the petrol to drive her daughter all over the North-East. Without her mum by her side, Beth's dream of becoming a footballer would never have come true. Now definitely wasn't the time to give up.

I've got to keep on making Mum proud, Beth resolved.

CHAPTER 22

GOLDEN GIRL

It was just before Christmas 2022 when the Mead family received an early present. It was a gift that confirmed Beth's incredible rise from footballer to national treasure after her Euros heroics that summer. A prize that was far beyond anything she had ever dreamed of.

Sports Personality of the Year was a show that Beth and her sports-mad family used to watch every year on TV when Beth and Ben were growing up. It was usually a male sports hero who won, and Beth couldn't remember a female footballer having ever been nominated. So, when the England star discovered that she had been shortlisted for the main prize, for once she was lost for words!

Beth and Viv went along to the TV studios in Salford for the glitzy ceremony on a chilly grey evening. Dad came too, while Mum tuned in back home in Hinderwell. Now in the final stages of a battle she could not win, Mum was all Beth could think about as she and Viv hobbled on their crutches down the red carpet outside the TV studios.

The Lionesses had been nominated for the Team of the Year too, as well as Sarina for the top coach award. Beth was excited to see some of her Lionesses teammates again – it seemed like a lifetime ago since Jill, Mary, Alessia, Lauren, Ellen, Ella and herself had last been together.

'You ladies look stunning,' Beth told her teammates as they found their seats together. 'I'm just glad they let me in wearing trainers!'

Jill laughed. 'Getting injured just so you wouldn't have to wear high heels, I don't know!'

So when Olympian Jessica Ennis-Hill announced that England Women had a new trophy to claim, tears of pride welled in Beth's eyes. She hobbled onto the stage behind her teammates to accept the prize, as Jill thanked the nation for supporting the Lionesses so brilliantly that summer.

The next award went to Sarina – 2022's Coach of the Year.

'Yesss!' yelled Beth, bursting with happiness. From the moment she'd met the Dutch master, Beth had known Sarina was a game-changer, an actual legend.

Could Beth make it a clean sweep of awards for the Lionesses? She was certainly favourite to win, but her stomach was now performing somersaults. What an honour it would be to join the list of some of the greatest heroes in sporting history.

Then at last the main award was decided:

Third place went to Eve Muirhead, a champion curler.

Second place and runner-up was Ben Stokes, England's cricket captain.

'The 2022 BBC Sports Personality of the Year is . . .' Dame Tanni Grey-Thompson read from the card. 'Beth Mead!'

Everyone in the audience rose to their feet to

give England's golden girl a standing ovation. Her incredible performances all year were an example to any young footballer growing up.

One last hug for luck with Dad, then Beth hobbled onto the stage again.

Hold it together. Hold it together, Beth told herself.

Cycling legend Chris Hoy presented Beth with the huge silver trophy, shaped like a TV camera.

'Wow, this is heavy!' Beth whispered to Chris.

She had a lot of people to thank, but her family were top of the list.

'I certainly wouldn't have done this without my dad, my mum and all my family,' she said, trying desperately to hold back the tears. She thanked her teammates for all their support too. 'Most of all this is for women's sport. Let's keep pushing, girls!'

Dramatic music began to play as ticker tape showered down. Beth was suddenly struck with emotion. Now the tears wouldn't stop. Soon, there was barely a dry eye in the house.

As Beth's rollercoaster year drew to a close, this was the most bittersweet moment of all. Tears of joy mingled with tears of such sadness. She knew this was the last Christmas present she would ever give her mum.

A text from Mum was waiting for Beth the next time she checked her phone. She picked out the words through tear-filled eyes: ECSTATIC! I LOVE YOU! SO PROUD!

'This is for you, Mum,' Beth replied.

CHAPTER 23

THE ROAD TO RECOVERY

Early in the new year, Beth got the call. The one she'd been expecting. The one she'd been dreading.

'Beth, you need to come home,' said Ben.

It was time. The doctors had done all they could.

It was calm, peaceful, beautiful even. A last chance to say: 'I love you'.

The days that followed were a blur. All Beth could remember was her, Dad and Ben, never wanting to let each other go.

A few days later, the time came to tell the world. Beth thought long and hard about what to write, but somehow words just didn't seem enough. She must have typed out the sentences and deleted them again a hundred times or more. Eventually, she settled on some lines that she hoped would do Mum justice. She chose some special photos too and held her breath as they uploaded.

Straightaway, the love began to pour out to Beth and her family from the whole football community. Her teammates at Arsenal and England, players and clubs from all over the world, and of course the fans. People whom she or Mum had never met sent their sympathies too, those who had lost loved ones to the same devastating disease.

Beth's old club Sunderland held a minute's silence before their match that Saturday, as did Arsenal who all wore black armbands too. June had been loved at both clubs, always singing along in the stands at her daughter's matches at the Hetton Centre and Meadow Park, where the two teams played their home games.

Arsenal's men shared a special tribute too after their North London derby victory at Tottenham Hotspur Stadium, holding up an Arsenal shirt to the cameras with 'THINKING OF YOU BETH' printed on the back and dedicating their victory to June.

Nothing could bring June back, but the amazing show of support brought comfort to the Mead family. Together, they got through the funeral.

*

Afterwards, Beth went back to London to carry on her rehab from injury. And carry on making her mum proud.

'We've got you,' her Arsenal teammates told her, on her first day back at London Colney. 'Whatever you need, we're here.'

And Beth knew it was true, that she could trust them 100 per cent. The girls and the staff were so full of kindness; Beth had never felt more loved. They had all known and loved June too. Their strength would be what would get Beth through the weeks and months ahead.

So Beth set to work on regaining her fitness. The physios had given her tasks to tick off each day. Gruelling weights in the gym. Workouts in the pool. And dips in the freezing ice bath. None of it was fun.

While some of the girls loved the gym, Beth had never been a fan. She'd rather be out on the pitch doing extra shooting practice or shuttle runs any day. Now, though, she had begun to find a strange comfort in the routine of the gym. Completing the same exercises, again and again, making baby steps on an exhausting journey.

It helped having Viv by her side, who was a few weeks behind Beth with the same lengthy recovery. They would pick each other up if they ever felt down.

With each week that passed, Beth could feel her knee starting to get stronger.

'We'll soon have you running again,' the physios told her. They were careful not to promise exactly when.

Even without a date to work towards, Beth felt strangely okay. *It will happen when it happens*, she told herself.

For now, the most important thing was being a good daughter to her dad, and a good sister to Ben, as well as looking after herself too. Football would still be there waiting, when she was ready to return. The last eighteen months had felt like riding a rollercoaster, with some of the highest highs and lowest lows of her whole life. Now she had been forced to slow down, she knew she had to learn to enjoy the ride.

There would be more twists and turns to come too. Good days and bad.

That's the thing about grief, Beth told herself. *One moment you feel like you've got this, the next it hits you with the force of a thousand crunching tackles.*

*

Beth was at home in St Albans when Sarina's squad for the Arnold Clark Cup was unveiled. It was the first England match that Beth would miss because of her injury.

The previous year, the Lionesses had been the surprise champions of the new mini tournament, beating Spain, Canada and Germany to the trophy. It had been a springboard for England's success that summer.

As the squad list flashed up on Sky Sports News, Beth's eyes scanned straight to see who would be wearing Number 7. For a fraction of a second, Beth half-expected to see her own name listed. *So silly!* 'CHLOE KELLY', it read.

Beth smiled. She was on the same journey now as Chloe had completed a year earlier – the Manchester City winger had recovered from her own ACL injury just in time to make the Euros squad. In a fairy-tale comeback, Chloe had gone on to score the goal that won England the tournament! Beth felt nothing but happiness for her teammate.

Meanwhile, the chances of Beth being back in time for the World Cup began to look slimmer. It would take a miracle to make the squad now, but Beth wasn't giving up.

'It's a long shot, but I'm pretty good at those!' she joked in an interview.

Even in tough times, Beth never stopped believing in herself and her ability – there was enough magic left in her boots for seasons yet to come. And if her comeback didn't happen in time for summer, a fresh season with Arsenal awaited afterwards.

'You heard it here first, everyone,' the presenter exclaimed. 'Meado's on her way back. She'll be terrifying defences again before we know it!'

Beth couldn't wait.

MEAD HONOURS

Sunderland

🏆 Women's Super League 2: 2014

🏆 Women's Premier League: 2011–12, 2012–13

🏆 Women's Premier League Cup: 2011–12

Arsenal

🏆 Women's Super League: 2018–19

🏆 Women's League Cup: 2017–18, 2022–23

England

🏆 UEFA Women's Championship: 2022

🏆 Arnold Clark Cup: 2022

🏆 SheBelieves Cup: 2019

Individual

- ♛ Member of the Order of the British Empire (MBE) for services to association football: 2023
- ♛ BBC Sports Personality of the Year: 2022
- ♛ BBC Women's Footballer of the Year: 2022
- ♛ UEFA Women's Championship 2022: Player of the Tournament, Golden Boot,
- ♛ Top Assist Provider, Team of the Tournament
- ♛ UEFA Women's Under-19 Championship Silver Boot: 2013
- ♛ World Soccer World Player of the Year: 2022
- ♛ England Player of the Year: 2021–22
- ♛ England Young Player of the Year: 2015, 2018
- ♛ WSL Player of the Season: 2015
- ♛ WSL Top Assist Provider: 2018–19, 2021–22
- ♛ WSL/WPL Golden Boot: 2011–12, 2012–13, 2015
- ♛ WSL Goal of the Season: 2018–19
- ♛ PFA Young Player of the Year: 2015–16
- ♛ PFA Young Player of the Year: 2015–16, 2017–18
- ♛ FSA Player of the Year: 2018, 2022
- ♛ Arsenal Player of the Season: 2021–22

- 🏆 Arsenal Supporters Club Player of the Season: 2017–18, 2021–22
- 🏆 Sunderland Forward of the Decade: 2011–2020
- 🏆 Sunderland Team of the Decade: 2011–2020
- 🏆 Sunderland Player of the Year: 2011–12, 2012–13, 2015–16
- 🏆 WSL Player of the Month: March 2019, April 2019, September 2021

MEAD

9

THE FACTS

NAME: Bethany Jane Mead

DATE OF BIRTH: 9 May 1995

PLACE OF BIRTH: Whitby, Yorkshire

NATIONALITY: English

BEST FRIEND: Jordan Nobbs

CURRENT CLUB: Arsenal

POSITION: Forward

THE STATS

Height (cm):	163
Club appearances:	248
Club goals:	117
Club trophies:	7
International appearances:	50
International goals:	29
International trophies:	3
Ballon d'Ors:	0

★ ★ ★ **HERO RATING: 96** ★ ★ ★

GREATEST MOMENTS

2011–12 SEASON, SUNDERLAND

In her first season with Sunderland, Beth finished as the league's top scorer with twenty-three goals in twenty-three games, as the Black Cats won the league and bagged the FA Women's Premier League Cup. Not bad for a sixteen-year-old!

19–31 AUGUST 2013,
UEFA WOMEN'S UNDER-19 CHAMPIONSHIP, WALES

Beth first shone on the European stage at the Under-19s Women's Euro 2013. Her goals helped the Young Lionesses go all the way to the final in Wales and won her the tournament's Silver Boot too. Nikita Parris and Katie Zelem were also in the squad.

27 FEBRUARY 2019,
ENGLAND 2–1 BRAZIL

Beth's famous 'crot', a cross-come-shot at the SheBelieves Cup in 2019 even had the American fans on their feet! She picked up a ball from Fran Kirby on the right wing, opened up her body and put her laces through the ball from a difficult angle. Beth was thrilled when she saw it hit top bins!

6 JULY 2022,
ENGLAND 1—0 AUSTRIA

Scoring the opening goal of the UEFA Women's Euro 2022 on home soil, in front of a packed crowd, is a strike that Beth is never likely to forget. She chested down another perfect pass from Fran before dinking the ball over the Austrian keeper and just over the goal line.

11 JULY 2022,
ENGLAND 8—0 NORWAY

Beth's three goals in England's demolition of Norway set the forward on her way to winning the Golden Boot at Euro 2022. Her first was a rare header, before beating a defender and finishing coolly in the corner for her second, while she completed her hat-trick with a tap-in!

TEST YOUR KNOWLEDGE

QUESTIONS

1. Which hobby did Beth try out before taking up football?

2. Which youth team in the North-East did Beth play for?

3. How old was Beth when she made her senior debut for Sunderland?

4. Beth shared the same journey from Middlesbrough to Sunderland to Arsenal as which of her England teammates?

5. Which Dutch player swiped Beth's spot as striker for Arsenal?

6. In which year did Beth make her debut for the senior Lionesses?

7. Beth played in her first Women's World Cup in 2019, but in which country was it held?

8. Which international competition did Beth miss out on in 2021?

9. How many goals did Beth score at UEFA Women's Euro 2022?

10. Which top European nation did England beat in the final of the same tournament?

11. Against which country did Beth win her fiftieth cap for the Lionesses?

Answers below . . . No cheating!

1. *Ballet.* 2. *Middlesbrough.* 3. *Sixteen.* 4. *Jordan Nobbs.* 5. *Vivianne Miedema.* 6. *2018.* 7. *France.* 8. *Women's Olympic Football Tournament, Tokyo 2020 (played in 2021).* 9. *Six goals, plus five assists!* 10. *Germany.* 11. *Japan.*

PLAY LIKE YOUR HEROES

THE BETH MEAD
SCHOOL OF FINISHING

STEP 1: To become a goalscoring great like Beth, you'll need to work on your finishing. She's not called the 'Hinderwell Hotshot' for nothing! Practise taking shots at goal from every angle, using both feet until you can't remember which was once your stronger foot.

STEP 2: It's useful to break down the different techniques involved in shooting to give you the best chance of scoring. Use your laces (the top of your boot where the laces usually are) to generate power in your shot.

STEP 3: The instep, or arched part at the top of foot between the laces and side of the foot, can be used to add curl, when making contact just below the centre of the ball. Lock your ankle and point your toes upwards when you hit the ball, to create enough spin to beat the keeper.

STEP 4: A volley is when a player strikes the ball first-time, as it's dropping out of the air. If it bounces before the player hits it, or they strike it on the bounce, it's called a half volley. Get your body into position, while watching the flight of the ball. Time your connection just right and your shot will be tough to stop. Top tekkers!

STEP 5: A toe-poke finish isn't the classiest, but it can get the ball over the line quickest in a goalmouth scramble – just ask Chloe Kelly! This shot is as it sounds – you use the front part of your boot where your toes are to connect with the ball.

STEP 6: Using the inside of your foot to place the ball produces less power, but gives you more accuracy. Try using this finish if you're close to the goal, or when you're in a tight space. As you approach the ball, turn your foot to the side before taking your shot. Boom!

STEP 7: A headed finish often follows a corner, free kick, cross or throw-in, when the ball is in the air. Remember to follow guidelines according to how old you are and practise your headers using soft or sponge footballs. Keeping your eyes on the ball, connect with it at the highest part of your jump using the centre of your forehead. Use your whole upper body to create the power you need.